NOTES &
QUERIES

VOLUME 2

NOTES & QUERIES

VOLUME 2

compiled by

Brian Whitaker

illustrations by

David Austin

FOURTH ESTATE · *London*

First published in Great Britain in 1991 by
Fourth Estate Limited
289 Westbourne Grove
London W11 2QA

Reprinted 1992, 1993

A catalogue record for this book is available from the British
Library

ISBN 1-872180-34-5

Typeset by York House Typographic Ltd, London
Printed and bound in Great Britain by
Cox & Wyman Ltd, Reading, Berkshire

PREFACE

THE AGE of Enlightenment began one Monday morning in November 1989 when Notes & Queries first appeared as a column in *The Guardian*. The idea was to provide a forum where readers could ask questions that are difficult to look up in conventional reference books – and invite other readers to answer them.

The questions, of course, are not the sort that would have troubled Mr Gorbachev during his enforced holiday in the Crimea, nor the sort that Magnus Magnusson torments his victims with as they sit under the spotlight, but the sort that occur to the rest of us at odd moments: perhaps while driving to work or taking a bath. Questions so bizarre, so perverse, so totally trivial – and yet so relentlessly persistent – that they refuse to go away.

It is on these questions that the weekly Notes & Queries column (and this collection in book form) attempts to provide enlightenment.

Readers with a mathematical bent will be quick to point out that the answers outnumber the questions. No doubt they will argue (as some did after the first volume appeared) that so many different answers can't all be right. That, if I may say so, is exactly the point: there are none of the boring certainties that you find in encyclopedias. Which of the answers in Notes & Queries are 'right' is a matter for readers themselves to decide. Enlightenment, indeed.

Brian Whitaker

QUESTION: If trapped in a plummeting lift, what is the best position to assume to minimise injury?

☐ THE SAFEST position is one where the legs are slightly bent, rather than braced. Survival depends on the length of drop, of course, but at least this position ensures that the thigh bones are not driven upwards into the abdominal cavity. Jumping upwards to reduce damage is not recommended, for three reasons. First, it is very difficult to time, and could worsen the situation if you land on the floor of the lift in an uncontrolled way. Second, by the time you have thought about this tactic you will already have impacted. Third, if you have time to think about this, and act on it, you have already fallen too far to survive. As a survivor of a drop in an ancient goods-lift back in 1962 (three-and-a-half floors with a load of two tons of chewing gum) I have to warn your readers that all is not yet over with the first impact. Close inspection of the bottom of lift shafts reveals a series of springs designed to absorb energy. This energy has to be expressed in some way, and in this case it has the effect of propelling the lift back up the shaft. You will return up the shaft with a slightly reduced velocity to that with which you descended only a few seconds ago. At the top of your rise you will experience an instant *déjà vu* as you descend again. After approximately five repetitions of this experience you will come to rest. Thus you will have plenty of time to practise any position which comes to mind, consider the nature of human existence, or just let blind terror take over. After this you can consider the next problem: how to get out of the wreckage. I am happy to say that I emerged uninjured but shaken. Others have not been so lucky.
Stephen Lutman, Faversham, Kent.

☐ ANY POSITION you adopt depends on the early recognition that the lift is in free-fall. For this reason you should always carry a set of bathroom scales which you can stand on in the lift. You should of course ignore the initial drop in weight as the lift begins a normal descent, but you should then watch avidly in case the reading approaches zero for more than a second. Having established that all is not well, your safest position is on top of the other occupants of the lift. One should therefore never travel in a lift less than half full, and if the choice exists one should choose fellow passengers who are overweight. This not only offers the greatest cushion on impact but generally they are less mobile when fighting for position.

Peter Jackson, Prees, Shropshire.

QUESTION: What makes my brass earrings go dull, and why does dipping them in HP Sauce for a few minutes have a rejuvenating effect?

☐ BRASS is an alloy of copper and zinc. In air, the copper tarnishes, becoming covered with a thin brown film of oxide (from atmospheric oxygen) or sulphide (from pollutants containing sulphur). On prolonged exposure to town air, a green film of the basic sulphate (verdigris) is formed, caused by sulphur dioxide in the atmosphere. HP Sauce contains a fair amount of acetic acid as a constituent of vinegar and in this dilute form it will dissolve, or at least render partially soluble, the thin films of copper oxide, sulphide, basic sulphate, etc, leaving the earrings nice and shiny. And it's cheaper than Brasso, too.

Peter Finan, Bradford, W. Yorks.

☐ NEVER mind *why* dipping them in HP Sauce has a rejuvenating effect: how did the questioner discover that it does?

Neil Harding, Pwllheli, Gwynedd.

☐ IN South-East Asia tamarind or an infusion of tamarind is used to clean brass. HP Sauce contains tamarind.

R. Yaacob, London SE5.

QUESTION: Why do the stripes on British men's ties run down from right to left (as you look at them), whereas American stripes run down left to right?

☐ ALTHOUGH the art of heraldry is dead, its original purpose of identifying a group of people with a common interest lives on in men's ties. The Club, the Old School, the Regiment, all produce their symbol of unity, sometimes bearing a shield or a simple device such as a raven or a lion. The stripe on ties is the equivalent of the heraldic bend, which is a charge on a shield consisting of a diagonal band drawn from the top right hand side to the bottom left (or from the dexter chief to the sinister base in heraldic terms). In heraldry the bend was sometimes reversed, from sinister chief to dexter base. This is called the 'bend sinister' and implies bastardy. I leave my American friends to explain why they have chosen this device.
J. Douglas Perret, Datchet, Berks.

☐ STRIPES on British ties slope from the wearer's left shoulder down towards the right, which follow the line of a double-breasted jacket (buttoning left over right). Only a few English regimental ties deviate from this rule; that of the Artists' Rifles is one, perhaps as an indication of their creative licence. The reason why American ties do not follow this harmonious design is that British fabric cutters traditionally work with their fabric face up, while Americans cut theirs face down, which reverses the design. But as one of the most popular designs of ties in the US is in the colours of the Argyll & Sutherland Highlanders, the difference in direction is also a handy indication of those actually entitled to wear particular ties and those Americans who simply like their colours.
Paul Keers (author of A Gentleman's Wardrobe*), London W1.*

☐ BRITISH ties are described as High Right; US as Reverse

Bias. President Bush favours British High Right ties from
Savile Row.
Kathryn Flett, London W12.

□ AN INTERESTING game is to spot TV personalities with ties
bought in America. Peter Snow and Martyn Lewis are two
recent examples.
Jack Griffiths, Worthing, W. Sussex.

**QUESTION: There are green insects, green reptiles and
green birds, but no green mammals. Why?**

□ THERE ARE in fact green mammals: the two-toed sloth and
three-toed sloth (*Choloepus* and *Bradypus* spp). However,
these are not truly green, but have specially adapted grooves
in the hairs of their fur to which cling a blue-green algae
(*cyanophyta*). The algae give the overall appearance of
green fur. As students of behavioural ecology, we cannot
envisage an adaptive reason for the lack of green mammals.
We would like to suggest a physiological constraint on the
pigmentation of mammalian hair.
*Philip Bateman, Fiona Clarke, and Emma Creighton, the
Open University, Milton Keynes.*

□ THE GREEN coloration of reptiles and birds is a mixture of
yellow and blue. The yellow is a pigment, while the blue is a
refraction effect called Tyndall blue, produced by transparent particles dispersed in a transparent medium with a
different refractive index. Tyndall blue can and does appear
in eyes, scales, feathers, and skin, where there are transparent substances of uniform texture, in which minute air
bubbles or other transparent particles may occur. It cannot
appear in hair which is never uniform in texture but always
consists of stringy bundles. We can imagine mammals with
green skin, made by adding a yellow pigment to the Tyndall
blue of a mandrill's cheeks, but it is difficult to imagine a

selective advantage for them. Green is a camouflage colour, not a signal colour. To be useful to a mammal, it needs to be in the hair.
Donald Rooum, London SW2.

☐ THERE is another way in which mammals can be green, besides mixing a yellow pigment with a blue produced by the Tyndall effect. A mixture of black and yellow gives a dull green colour, which might make a better camouflage than the brighter greens produced by the blue-yellow mix. We cannot think of many species of mammals which are green because they mix yellow and black but some squirrel monkeys have an olive-green appearance by having black tips to yellowish hairs.
Peter Cotgreave, Arne Mooers and Andy Purvis, Department of Zoology, University of Oxford.

QUESTION: If mercury is such a problem as a pollutant and a poison, how is it that many of us can have it stuffed into cavities in our teeth without any question as to its safety?

☐ IT IS highly improbable that the mercury in dental amalgam can cause poisoning, as it is combined chemically with the other metals in the mix, chiefly silver and tin. This means that it cannot form vapour, which is one of the most poisonous phases of mercury. No other filling material can surpass amalgam in terms of its long-term wear and sealing properties.
(Ms) E. R. Denning (BDS), Rowney Green, near Alvechurch, Birmingham.

☐ IT IS all very well Ms Denning (BDS) trying to put our minds at rest but . . . when a dentist squeezes amalgam into a patient's cavity small droplets of mercury frequently appear, even sometimes popping down their throats. And

that is not all . . . when drilling out old mercury amalgam, mercury vapour is sometimes released. Are there any known cases of mercury poisoning? I think we should be told.
Alan Phillips, Dean of Information Services, Birmingham Polytechnic.

QUESTION: Why was it that, though Renaissance painters could turn out such wonderful works of art, they could not depict a baby which looked like a baby? The Virgin and Child were a common subject but the child was usually completely misshapen and out of all proportion.

□ THE QUESTION seems to have been answered by Leonardo da Vinci: '. . . for instance, those who represent a one-year-old boy with the proportions of a man of 30, giving the body eight headlengths instead of five. They have so often committed this error and seen it committed so often, that they have become used to it, and the habit has lodged itself so deeply in their corrupt judgment that they make themselves believe that Nature, or whoever imitates Nature, are gravely wrong when they deviate from this practice.' [Quoted by Sir

Ernst Gombrich, in his Richard Bradford Lecture, *Proceedings of the Royal Institution of Great Britain*, vol 52, pp 113-144 (1980).] Figures 9 and 10 in Gombrich's lecture illustrate the questioner's point rather well.
Ivor Williams, Royston, Herts.

QUESTION: Is it possible to construct a sentence (in English) in which every letter of the alphabet is used once and once only? Vladimir Nabokov is reported to have promised John Updike half the royalties to *Lolita* if he could do it, but apparently he failed. Can anyone else do better?

☐ THE CHAPTER on the pangram (a sentence containing all the letters of the alphabet) in my book, the *Oxford Guide to Word Games,* includes several examples of such sentences. Some cheat by using initials, such as 'Blowzy night-frumps vex'd Jack Q' and 'J Q Schwartz flung V D Pike my box.' Others resort to unusual words: 'Cwm fjord-bank glyphs vext quiz' means that an eccentric was annoyed to see ancient inscriptions on the side of a fjord in a valley.
Tony Augarde, Oxford University Press, Oxford.

☐ 'JUMP, dogs! Why vex Fritz Blank, QC?' Does anyone claim copyright on this? Or can I have half the royalties to *Lolita?*
(Rev.) Sydney Knight, Elvington, York.

☐ MICHAEL Jones of Chicago once described a wryneck woodpecker from the African grasslands climbing the side of a male bovid grazing on sacred Muslim-owned land as 'Veldt jynx grimps waqf zho buck'. This is somewhat contrived but could be usefully recalled when playing Scrabble.
Tony Abramson, Leeds.

☐ *THE GUINNESS Book of Records* credits Paul Horn of New

York with the creation of the most intelligible 26-letter pangram: 'Mr Jock, TV quiz PhD, bags few lynx'.
Russ Swan, Nottingham

QUESTION: Could somebody confirm or scotch for all time that enduring rumour concerning everlasting light bulbs, the patent of which was supposedly bought by an unscrupulous manufacturer so that they could never be produced?

☐ YOU MIGHT like to consider the idea of everlasting light bulbs from the economist's, rather than the engineer's, point of view. During the 1970s the industry was subject to investigation by the Monopolies & Mergers Commission. As a result the industry was ordered to manufacture long-lasting bulbs. These were launched with a great deal of advertising ballyhoo and at a suitably inflated price. The demise of these highly dangerous(!) products was assured by shops not selling them and the manufacturers not supplying them. Thus, all we had was an advertising campaign. After a while the industry was able to report to the MMC that there was no demand. This is an interesting illustration of the argument put forward by J. K. Galbraith in *The New Industrial State*. He maintains that the chief function of a monopolies commission is to be seen to be doing something about monopolies but it must on no account actually do anything. Occasionally the commission may deal severely with small and unimportant business – cast-iron drainpipes is an example which springs to mind. On no account must it interfere with the chief industrial, commercial or financial monopolies. I'm afraid you will have to wait a long time for an everlasting light bulb.
John Beardshaw, Puckeridge, Herts.

☐ I FIRST heard this story nearly 40 years ago, and it was old then. A patent, especially one not being exploited, could last

for only 16 years in those days, so it must have run out well over 20 years ago, if the story were true. This means that anyone could exploit the invention. So it was not the patent that prevented the everlasting light bulb from being made. I suspect that it was never invented.
K. J. A. Crampton, Brockenhurst, Hants.

☐ I CAN happily scotch the enduring rumour. The life of light bulbs can be prolonged by manufacturing them with thicker filaments but even then they don't last for ever and, worse still, they become energy guzzlers, the thicker the filament. The nearest thing in real life to an everlasting bulb is a compact fluorescent lamp which lasts eight times as long as an ordinary light bulb and uses only 20 per cent of the electricity to produce the same amount of light, so it is enviromentally friendly. These can be bought from the larger multiple retailers, DIY outlets and local electricity boards. Remember, the major cost of lighting is not the bulb but the electricity it consumes.
Ernest Magog, Director, Lighting Industry Federation, London SW17.

☐ IT IS curious that when 'explaining' the limitation on the life of a light bulb, the director of the Lighting Federation focuses on an irrelevance – the thickness of the filament – and not the true problem, the degree of vacuum. Filaments break because they oxidise. Replacing all the air with an inert gas would prevent this. Manufacturers obviously won't admit they leave some air in the bulb.
Rod Burnham, St Paul's Cray, Kent.

☐ IT IS difficult to say exactly what is everlasting in respect to such a relatively new product as a light bulb. However, in the Edison Museum in Fort Myers, Florida, there are bulbs in daily use which have been there for 70 or 80 years and were among the early products of Edison. I have a feeling

that the filaments are made of bamboo rather than the tungsten which is currently used.
G. N. Hall, Kew Gardens, Surrey.

☐ THE RADIAL tyre clearly refutes the rumour that the everlasting light bulb, non-laddering stockings and other such items have been suppressed by manufacturers keen to stay in business. Designed originally to cope with the exceptionally high wear of Citroën's front-wheel-drive cars, the radial tyre became widely adopted by tyre-makers around the world. They last at least three times as long as conventional crossply tyres and have caused a massive restructuring of the global tyre industry – with the demise of Dunlop being the most significant development here in UK. Much of the former Dunlop empire is now controlled by Sumitomo Rubber of Japan or the giant conglomerate BTR plc (which itself, originally Birmingham Tyre and Rubber, moved out of tyres at the start of the 'radial revolution'). I think this clearly shows that you can be sure of one thing in this world of market economies: if someone, somewhere can make something cheaper, better or long-lasting, someone will do it. In any case, there are longer-lasting conventional light bulbs available: they cost more to buy and use significantly more energy, so that total savings over their lifetimes are minimal. Even so, they were/are widely used when the cost of replacing a bulb is significant. More recently, however, lights have become available based on the fluorescent principle which last much longer and consume much less energy. Although they cost more, because they are more expensive to make, total savings over their lifetimes are significant enough to make their use attractive to ordinary domestic users. The film, *The Man in the White Suit*, was an entertaining look at the problems that an everlasting cloth would create in Britain's textile industry. Unfortunately, the world's tyre-makers and their employees found the experience a lot more painful.
D. R. Reed and colleagues at the European Rubber Journal, *London.*

QUESTION: I have been told that the *Magic Roundabout* **was originally a French political satire with each character representing a figure in French politics. Apart from guessing Dougal as De Gaulle, who are the others?**

☐ FRENCH politicians? I find that hard to swallow. Those of us at a certain age know that the *Magic Roundabout* was an Early Learning introduction to drug culture: 'It's a marvellous feeling,' Mr Rusty told Dougal about a 'trip' on his roundabout. A staple part of common-room conversation was to identify the illegal substance that each character represented. Many years and several flashbacks later, I now find it difficult to recall what they were . . . ah, let me see. Florence was a more butch version of our Alice, an innocent abroad; Dylan, the hippy bunny, was hashish; Brian was amphetamines. But what substance was produced from those flowers Ermintrude kept chewing, that once made her triple her size and fly away? And Dougal? At the time I thought his supply of sugar cubes had something to do with LSD but now I'm not so sure. Personally I'd like to know if there is any truth in the rumour that the BBC has banned it from our screens. Anyhow, time for bed.
Martin Ridgwell, Manchester 16.

☐ I THINK the questioner is wrong in saying that the *Magic Roundabout (Le Manège Enchanté)* was a political satire in Serge Danot's original French version. It was a simple children's series in which Dougal was called Pollux and spoke French with a heavy English accent (the French never fail to find an English accent hugely amusing). The rabbit was called Flappy and spoke with a heavy Spanish accent (the French people's other joke). Brian, the snail, was called Ambroise and Florence was Margote. There was no subtlety in the stories compared to the sophisticated version produced later for English TV by Eric Thompson. Hardly any

adults watched it except English expats living in Paris at the time who used Pollux's sayings as catchphrases (at least they could manage that accent).
J. Cormack, Leicester.

QUESTION: **I understand that the pungency (heat) of chilli peppers is measured in Scoville Heat Units. Where can I look this up?**

□ OF THE hundreds of different kinds of chilli grown around the world, only a few varieties are available in the UK. Pungency depends on the amount of capsaicin present and the degree of heat is measured in Scoville units (named after W. L. Scoville). In his book, *Spices and Herbs For the Food Industry* (Food Trade Press, 1984), Dr Y. S. Lewis gives examples of both the capsaicin content and the Scoville heat value of some chilli varieties, ranging from the Mombasa of Africa (100,000 Scoville units) to the milder Mexico (40,000 Scoville units). Commercially ground chilli powder is typically between 8,000 and 10,000 Scoville units. Because of its potential combustibility, chilli needs to be processed (cleaned and ground) with considerable caution. In 1989, a chilli warehouse in Los Angeles was destroyed by spontaneous combustion, destroying $70,000 of stock. Capsaicin is fat soluble but not water soluble. This explains why drinking water will not help a burnt chilli mouth, but milk or yogurt will.
Hillary Box, Indian Spices Information Bureau, London WC1.

□ THE SCOVILLE scale was devised in 1912, and 1 per cent of capsaicin is equivalent to 150,000 Scoville Heat Units. See *Cooking With Spices* by Carolyn Heal and Michael Alsop (Panther Books, 1985).
(Dr) Jeremy Bartlett, Norwich.

QUESTION: What were the original Satanic Verses, alluded to in the title of Salman Rushdie's novel?

☐ MECCA in the year 610 (when the Prophet Muhammad began receiving revelations from Allah) was a bustling city, whose only sources of legal income were commerce and the trade engendered by pilgrimages to the pagan temple in Mecca – the Ka'ba. This temple was crammed to the roof with images of the main Meccan deities: Allah, and his daughters and consorts, Al-Lat, Al-Uzza and Manat. According to a little-disseminated Muslim tradition, when first the Prophet began preaching monotheism publicly to the largely pagan populace, he came under tremendous pressure to say something which would allow the pagans to convert smoothly to Islam without loss of face. (If this sounds reprehensible, consider the motives of the early Christian missionaries to Britain, who built their chapels and churches over sacred pagan sites.) During this period, Muhammad is said to have passed on a revelation, believing it to have come from Allah, which said something like: 'Have you considered Al-Lat and Al-Uzza and Manat, the third, the other? Those are the exalted swans. Their intercession is expected. Their likes are not neglected.' On hearing this, many pagans converted to Islam. When Muhammad realised what he had said, he claimed that the Devil – Shaytan – had put these verses into his mouth to discredit him. He then passed on the real revelation from Allah, which can be found in Sura 53 ('The Star') of the Qur'an. In the Arberry version (OUP £2.95), the amended revelation reads: 'Have you considered Al-Lat and Al-Uzza and Manat, the third, the other? What, have you males and He females? That were indeed an unjust division.They are naught but names yourselves have named, and your fathers; God has sent down no authority touching them.' When the recent converts heard the new, Allah-given version, they were furious: they believed that they had been tricked into converting. Their

persecution of Muhammad and his genuine, committed converts now redoubled.
Sandra Poole, Altrincham, Cheshire.

QUESTION: Whatever became of the Flat Earth Society?

☐ MY MATHS teacher once told my class that he was the last remaining member of the Flat Earth Society, after a successful voyage by all the other members to find the edge of the earth.
Timothy Dale, Byker, Tyneside.

☐ THERE ARE a few Flat Earth societies still operating in various parts of the world, for example in California and in India, but the original Flat Earth Society launched here in England effectively ceased to function in the mid-1970s, after the death of Sam Shenton, its long-time mainspring and advocate. There are still Flat Earth believers in this country, but to the best of my knowledge they are without an organisation to help them publicise their beliefs. Through the good offices of Ellis Hillman, a councillor of the defunct Greater London Council, the Science Fiction Foundation obtained from Mrs Shenton her late husband's literary effects. The collection is available for viewing and research to any bona fide inquirer. Applications to view the collection should be made in term-time to the Administrator, The Science Fiction Foundation, Polytechnic of East London, Longbridge Road, Dagenham, RM8 2AS. Tel 081 590 7722.

Charles Barren, Past-Chairman, The Science Fiction Foundation, Gravesend, Kent.

□ FOLLOWING the death of Mr Shenton in 1962, Patrick Moore, the astronomer, strongly argued against dissolving the society. It is now essentially a society for challenging 'scientific orthodoxy' in the style of its late Victorian and Edwardian predecessors, the Zatetic Society and the London Dialectical Society. Although the society is subterranean and somewhat elusive, it has managed to deliver lectures at Oxford Polytechnic, Portsmouth Polytechnic and Liverpool University. Perhaps its most notable success was its intervention at the Oxford University Scientific Society where a motion that 'This house believes that the earth is flat' was carried unanimously.

Ellis Hillman, Hendon, London NW4.

□ THE FLAT EARTH Society lives on, growing in influence and eccentricity since its change of name. It is now known as the Adam Smith Institute.

John Nicholls, Cranfield, Beds.

MEXICAN ROULETTE

QUESTION: When police and soldiers fire their guns into the air to disperse crowds, what happens to the bullets? Are they still potentially lethal?

☐ THIS is not just a theoretical danger. In the Philippines, dozens of people are injured, some killed, every New Year's Eve due to the tradition of firing guns in the air at midnight. Most embassies in Manila recommend that their nationals stay indoors, preferably on a lower floor, during the festivities.
Bob Couttie, Manila, Philippines.

☐ BULLETS come down with just about as much speed as they go up, less a little for air resistance; Galileo worked this out in relation to cannonballs. Police and soldiers may, if you're lucky, use blanks. More commonly they rely on the hope that the crowd is fairly small in relation to the total area within which the bullets might fall. This does break down with large crowds. One ironic instance occurred in Pakistan during the celebrations of Benazir Bhutto's wedding: men within the crowd fired their guns skywards in celebration and there were reports of at least one woman dying as the result of bullets falling back. During the Second

World War, people were killed when debris from their own side's anti-aircraft shells fell on them.
Humphrey Evans, London N7.

☐ IT IS nonsense to say that they come down as fast as they go up. A modern rifle round can reach 1,000mph. Once its upward climb is spent, it is subject to gravity, accelerating it down at 9.7mps, until air resistance steadies its velocity. Doubtless a smart rap on the skull, but barely lethal. Casualties from anti-aircraft fire are from unexploded shells (faulty fuse) coming back down. Though the time fuse has failed, the impact fuse usually works.
Jeremy Haworth, Cardiff.

☐ A BULLET fired in the air will indeed behave as Jeremy Haworth suggests, assuming the 'mps' is a misprint for m/s/ s. But, if the muzzle velocity were 1,000mph (447mps) and the mass of the bullet were 10gm, the initial energy level would be no less than 1,000 Joule. Even allowing as much as a 90 per cent loss of energy during flight (due to air friction) we are left with 100 Joule and a velocity of 141mps (315mph). A smart rap on the skull? Try this one: drop a 50gm golf ball on your noddle from a height of 1m. It will arrive at a velocity of about 4.5mps (10mph) with a total energy of about 0.5 Joule. When your howls of agony have subsided, ponder on the effect of 100 Joule.
R. H. Ellis, Sutton, Surrey.

QUESTION: Why are 'square' biscuit tins not actually square? The lids only fit one way round.

☐ THIS is to enable the empty tins to be packed more efficiently when being transported to the bakery. If the tins were square, they would have to be packed separately, one on top of the other. As each tin would be empty, this would

mean that the lorry was carrying more empty space than
tins. Because they are slightly oblong, it is possible to stand
two tins on their short edge inside another tin and then use a
fourth tin as a lid, which means you can now carry four tins
in the space that would previously only hold two. Therefore
the number of lorries needed to deliver a consignment of tins
is instantly halved. Clever!
Chris Quinn, Huyton, Merseyside.

**QUESTION: How did medical research stumble upon
the fact that nitro-glycerine [an explosive] is a useful
vasodilator?**

☐ THE distinguished pharmacologist and physician, Thomas Lauder Brunton, introduced into late 19th-century
clinical practice the use of amyl-nitrite for the relief of the
pain of angina pectoris. He had seen others use it in humans
and in animal experiments to reduce blood pressure, and
reasoned that it might be effective for patients suffering
from an acute anginal attack. The rapid symptomatic relief
produced by 'this remarkable substance', as Brunton
reported to the *Lancet* in 1867, stimulated studies on related
chemicals and in 1879 William Murrell wrote to the *Lancet*
of the beneficial effects of nitro-glycerine. The production of
this chemical by the Nobel explosives factory from the mid-
1860s onwards made it readily available for therapeutic use,
although its identity was frequently concealed from patients
under chemical synonyms such as glyceryl-trinitrate. It is
absorbed rapidly, especially from the sub-lingual mucosa,
and pharmaceutical preparations are usually tablets to be
put under the tongue or aerosol sprays. It can also be
absorbed through the skin: and individuals employed in the
manufacture of explosives may suffer from headaches, diz-
ziness and other symptoms during their first few days
exposure, but rapidly tolerate the pharmacological effects.

Absence from the stimulus can cause the tolerance to lessen, instigating a new attack of 'Monday disease'.
(Dr) Tilli Tansey, Wellcome Institute for the History of Medicine, London, WC1.

QUESTION: Why are the lecterns in Anglican churches almost always in the form of an eagle with outspread wings?

☐ THE FLYING eagle is the symbol of John the Evangelist (see Revelation, ch 4 v 7) who proclaimed Christ as 'the Word of God' at the beginning of his Gospel. The flying eagle is thus a suitable emblem from which God's word is read, reaching (we hope) the ends of the earth. The eagle is also thought of as the bird which flies nearest to heaven. I am not sure such lecterns are confined just to the Anglican church. It was not until the Reformation that the lectern became prominent in ordinary parish churches of the reformed tradition, carrying the open bible. Reformed churches other than the Anglican have perhaps eschewed this type of lectern as a 'graven image'. Since Vatican II the Roman Catholic church has made the bible reading more prominent in the services, but the lectern used is likely to be of a light, moveable sort.
Rev. Harold Webb, Guildford, Surrey.

☐ IT'S a matter of a pinion.
Peter Barnes, Milton Keynes.

☐ THIS predates the Anglican church by several centuries and goes back at least as far as the early medieval use of astrological symbols in church design. The eagle of Scorpio is one of the four fixed signs of the zodiac and they represented stability and endurance long before Christianity was invented. They were appropriated to symbolise the four Apostles who were considered to be the firm and lasting foundation of the Church. Leo was given to Mark, Scorpio to

John, Taurus to Luke and Aquarius to Matthew. In esoteric astrology the eagle replaces the scorpion as a sign of Scorpio's ability to be spiritually reborn, rising above earthly desires; divine inspiration is ascribed to Leo and the potential divinity of mankind to Aquarius. Taurus represents the voice of God and so was often omitted from the design, as it was left to the preacher to fulfil this role. Further insights on the occult roots of Christian symbols can be found in Fred Gettings' book, *The Hidden Art*.

Hilary Scott, Teignmouth.

QUESTION: Many towns in France have a Rue Gambetta or a Place Gambetta. Who was Gambetta?

☐ LEON GAMBETTA (1838–82) is perhaps best remembered for his heroic, if futile, attempt to raise the siege of Paris during the Franco-Prussian war of 1870–71.. A radical republican lawyer of Italo-French extraction, Gambetta had proclaimed the Third Republic in September 1870 after the defeat and abdication of Napoleon II, and became Minister of the Interior in the government of National Defence. On October 7, 1870, he escaped from Paris by balloon to Tours, where he formed a conscript army to march on the capital. After some initial success, the rabble was split and defeated. Gambetta, now Minister of War, decamped with the government to Bordeaux. However, after the fall of Paris in January 1871, the government made peace and Gambetta resigned. He played a pivotal role in the Third Republic over the next 10 years, denouncing conservatism and supporting colonial expansion, and was briefly prime minister in 1881. His belief in revenge ('Always to think of it and never to say it') and anti-clericalism ('Clericalism is the enemy') struck chords among his countrymen and may account for his enduring popularity. He died in 1882 from wounds sustained in an accident with a revolver.

John Duffy, Wallasey, Merseyside.

☐ HE was a one-eyed Liberal Republican who to his credit argued against the persecution of the Paris communards. We have a Gambetta Street in Battersea. Once Wandsworth Council realise this they'll probably rename it after Jean-Marie Le Pen.
John O'Farrell, London SW8.

QUESTION: Apparently the 'HP' in HP Sauce stands for the Houses of Parliament. But why?

☐ IN the late 1890s Samson Moore was a prosperous vinegar brewer. His ambition was to manufacture a sauce that would become a household name. When he visited Mr F. G. Garton of Nottingham trying to recover a business debt he discovered that he was brewing a home-made sauce that 'smelled uncommonly good'. Attached to the basket cart was a board with the sign 'Garton's HP Sauce'. When asked for an explanation of the letters HP, Mr Garton replied he had heard a faint rumour that a bottle of his sauce had been seen in a restaurant at the Houses of Parliament. Within minutes Mr Garton's debt had been cancelled and he was paid £150 for the name and the recipe. Further information available in *The True Story of HP Sauce* by Dinsdale Landen and Jennifer Daniel.
Alan W. Brown, Edinburgh.

QUESTION: Do spiders urinate in the manner we are usually acquainted with; in fact, are there any animals which don't?

☐ HOWEVER spiders may urinate, I hope they undo their flies first.
Peter Barnes, Milton Keynes.

☐ ALL animals carry out processes corresponding to urination, but they do this in many different ways. The major functions are: removing products containing nitrogen, removing unwanted salts, and adjusting water balance. In man and mammals all three functions are carried out by the kidneys and a liquid urine is stored in a bladder before voiding. This is possible because water is available and nitrogenous waste is produced as urea, which is soluble and relatively non-toxic. Spiders and many insects convert nitrogenous waste to a very insoluble substance, uric acid, from which almost all water is removed before it is shed as a solid, and it may be argued that this is because they have to conserve water. But birds and flying insects with ready access to water, produce an almost dry 'urine' with uric acid, and it may be that reducing weight by eliminating a bladder containing water is the more important factor. The functions carried out by our kidneys may be separated in other creatures. Some remove salts by special 'salt glands'; fresh-water animals have continually to pump out excess water, and may make a virtue of necessity by discharging nitrogen-ous waste in the water as water dilutes ammonia, which would be poisonous if concentrated in a bladder. The pro-cess can change in the life of a single animal: the larva of a water beetle produces ammonia, but the flying adult changes to uric acid. Bee and ant lion larvae store up all their nitrogenous excreta and void it only when they become adult. One animal appears not to excrete nitrogen at all: the greenfly. It puts its nitrogenous waste in its offspring. At first sight this seems an impossible solution; but if it puts one 10th of its production in each of 10 offspring, and an offspring puts one tenth of its own production plus one tenth of the inherited material, i.e. one hundredth, in each of its children, and so on, it soon arrives at an almost constant load of insoluble uric acid. At the end of the summer aphids lay eggs, and the uric acid in the corpse is broken down and returned to plants from which they obtained the nitrogen in the first place.

(Sir) James Beament, Queen's College, Cambridge.

☐ THE MOST concentrated nitrogenous waste is produced by woodlice, which are terrestrial crustaceans. They puff gaseous ammonia into the atmosphere.
(Ms) Mo Killip, Cambridge.

QUESTION: In which play did a character say, 'Anyone for tennis?'

☐ I DON'T actually believe that there was a play in which a character uttered this cry. The originator of the phrase was none other than Humphrey Bogart. As a struggling actor in the 1920s, he went through a succession of small roles in off-Broadway plays. These roles, he claimed, consisted mainly of bounding on stage, tennis racket in hand, while asking the immortal question. The nearest he actually got to 'Anyone for tennis?' was 'Tennis anyone?' in a play that, unlike Bogart, vanished into obscurity.
Alan Diment, Poole, Dorset.

☐ IN Bernard Shaw's *Misalliance* (1910), Johnny Tarleton, son of a tycoon who has made a fortune out of manufacturing underwear, asks: 'Anybody for a game of tennis?'
G. E. Brown, Sidcup. Kent.

QUESTION: If Guy Fawkes had lit the gunpowder would it really have killed King and Parliament, or just given them a bit of a fright?

☐ THE SHORT answer is that the King and those with him would probably have been killed. Although superseded by more powerful explosives, black gunpowder was, by the time of the plot, sufficiently evolved to be a very dangerous commodity indeed. Ignited *en masse*, in a cellar, it would lack the shattering effect of modern high explosives but it would certainly have caused extensive demolition, probably

accompanied by fire. Black gunpowder is still a very popular explosive in quarries in various parts of the world.
Dr M. Rasburn (MRSC, C Chem), N Whittington, Chesterfield, Derbys.

QUESTION: What is the likely effect of the Earth's magnetic polarity reversing? Is it overdue?

☐ CHANGES in the Earth's magnetic field are known to have an effect on climate and changes in polarity have been associated with major changes in temperature, although a direct causal link has yet to be established. As it is, the pattern of magnetic reversal seems to be highly irregular. There have been at least 171 reversals in the past 80 million years and, about 45 million years ago, the reversal frequency doubled to a rate of five reversals per million years. Recent studies have provided evidence for five short-lived magnetic reversals during the past 470,000 years. The cause of a change in polarity would appear to be sudden convection plumes or surges in the Earth's molten core caused by alterations in the Earth's orbit. When these interact with the weak electric currents generated by the circulation of the ocean, it alters the rate at which heat is distributed over the globe. A strengthening magnetic field is associated with a cooling of the Earth, while weakening is linked to warming. Since the temperature trend was firmly downwards during the 1970s and early 1980s a reversal might signal the onset of a new ice age. The greenhouse effect, however, has thrown a spanner in the works and the situation is now less certain.
Mark Swindale, Isle of Arran.

☐ THE BIRDS certainly will not fly north. Polarity reversal of the Earth's magnetic field has happened many times during the time that birds have used it as a navigational clue and so they detect not polarity but the acute angle of the lines of force as they intersect with the Earth's surface. Magnetic

clues are only a small part of the migrants' navigational repertoire so, even when they are in turmoil, many migrants will be able to make their journeys safely. For instance, young birds detect the centre of rotation of the stars by watching their movement. Essential, because the wobbles of the Earth's axis would mean they were 47° out after 13,000 years if they were to take the Pole Star as north.
Chris Mead, British Trust for Ornithology, Tring, Herts.

QUESTION: I have a postcard of a chap in a long jacket holding some sheet music (circa 1925). It is captioned: 'Mr Enos Bacon, the Yorkshire Nightingale'. Who was Mr Bacon?

☐ MY GREAT uncle, Mr Enos Bacon, was born the son of a coal miner and was brought up in the village of Hoyland, near Barnsley, South Yorkshire. He began his working life as a miner at Hemingfield Colliery, but quickly decided that mining was not his vocation. He left the mines to become a 'school bobby' – otherwise known as a truant officer. In his leisure time he excelled at entertaining the public. He specialised in one-man shows reading poetry (he had published works on local people), impersonations and singing. He had a lovely falsetto voice and became known as the 'Yorkshire Nightingale'. He had religious inclinations and was accepted into the Methodist Ministry. This became his life's work, with entertaining the public as a sideline. He was much travelled, spending several years in South Africa and later in America. He was married three times and had several children. He spent his last few years in his native South Yorkshire where he died in his mid-seventies. One of his brothers, Mr Horace Bacon, is still alive and well, aged 98, living in Sheffield.
(Mr) J Bacon, Huddersfield, W. Yorks.

QUESTION: What is the meaning of life?

☐ IN DOUGLAS Adams's book, *The Hitch-hiker's Guide to the Galaxy*, we are informed that the computer, Deep Thought, ponders over a period of 7½ million years the question of the meaning of Life, the Universe and Everything. It is widely understood that this machine calculated the total answer to these three separate concepts as 42. Thus dividing 42 by three, it can be deduced that the meaning of life alone is 14. This, however, can only be assumed if the ratio of Life to both the Universe and Everything is 1: 1: 1.
Khairoun Abji (student at Luton VI Form College), Luton, Beds.

☐ WHAT WE do know with certainty is that we were not once, are now, and will not be again.
Brian Mendes, Bromley, Kent.

☐ LIFE is a sexually transmitted condition with a 100% mortality rate.
P. Mellor, Centre for Software Reliability, City University, London EC1.

☐ LIFE is not a linguistic item and hence has no meaning. The question makes as much sense as 'What is the meaning of lumbago?'
Graham Bryant, Nottingham.

☐ LIFE is an acronym invented by Mr Kenneth Baker: Let In Free Enterprise.
(Dr) P. V. Youle, New Milton, Hants.

☐ MY OLD pal Plotinus has it thus: 'If a man were to enquire of Nature the reason of her creative activity, and she were willing to give ear and answer, she would say, "Ask not, but understand in silence, even as I am silent and am not wont to speak".'
N.J. Crofton-Sleigh, Norwich.

□ THE *CONCISE Oxford Dictionary* states that life is a 'state of functional activity and continued change peculiar to organised matter and especially to the portion of it constituting an animal or plant before death.' God knows (*sic*).
Jeff Thirburn, Nuneaton, Warwickshire.

□ LIFE has no meaning related to an external frame of reference, only the meaning that you decide to give it. It follows that any such meaning given is as valid as any other for you, and any change is also up to you. Have fun being Cesare Borgia on Wednesdays and St Francis on Thursdays.
Brian Cattermole, Stevington, Beds.

□ BEFORE directing the questioner to the nearest dictionary or his local priest I would strongly advise that this is a question not to be asked, unless rhetorically. History shows that individuals who asked this of themselves or others are prone to insanity, alcoholism or other addictions, even visions of religious ecstasy: none of these help in the least with an answer, only offering a temporary palliative for the passing of life while it is being experienced, or in providing hope for the hopeless. Matters such as destiny, happiness and other connected issues only complicate the question and should not be dragged on to the stage of reasoning. The greatest minds that have ever lived have not come near to answering this question; choose what eschatology you will for now. The chances are that whichever one you adhere to, we have all got it wrong (if only fundamentalists knew as much). This is a great mystery and long may it remain so. There is something a little dull about the prospect of knowing everything and our humble brains are not wired for that prospect. Life is for living, surely.
James A. Oliver, London WC2.

□ ACCORDING to a BBC2 Horizon programme screened some months ago (not on April 1) the meaning of life may have something to do with the notion that the most important living entity on this planet, the Earth itself, may regulate various life forms within its confines in order to ensure its own survival. Thus, for example, although the sun is now very much hotter than it was at the dawn of life, the proportion of oxygen in the atmosphere has remained more or less constant at 21 per cent, any greater or lesser amount being catastrophic. This suggests some kind of self-regulating mechanism which may be provided by the gases, particularly from manure, of all living things. That would also explain various epidemics and natural disasters as Mother Earth controls the number of living creatures and thus the level and mixture of atmospheric gases. What the meaning of life is for Planet Earth is another matter.

D. Fisher, Maidenhead, Berks.

QUESTION: What caused the fluorescence in the sand of Dunkirk beach 50 years ago? Does it still occur?

□ IF THE 'fluorescence' on the beaches was a green flush which came and went on wet sand, disappearing especially when approached, it was almost certainly caused by the behaviour of swarms of the flatworm called *Convoluta roscoffensis*. This tiny flatworm, only about 2mm long, is bright green in colour since its body contains symbiotic green algae. It lives inter-tidally in wet sand on beaches in northern France, coming to the sand surface to expose the algae to sunlight and allow them to photosynthesise, the products of photosynthesis benefiting both plant and animal. The green patches caused by swarms of these flatworms disappear when approached because the flatworms react to disturbance by sliding rapidly into the sand. The phenomenon can still be seen on shores in Brittany, so unless increased pollution and/or human disturbance has caused a decline in *Convoluta roscoffensis* populations on other

northern beaches, or unless the range of the animal has contracted, there is little reason why it should not still occur.
R. S. Bowman, BSc, M Phil, Whitby, N. Yorks.

☐ *CONVOLUTA roscoffensis* is certainly very abundant in wet sand on beaches of Brittany, Normandy and the Channel Islands, but, to my knowledge, Dunkirk is beyond the northern limit of its distribution. However, I would be very interested to hear if anyone has definitively identified it at Dunkirk.
A. E. Douglas, Department of Zoology, University of Oxford, OX1 3PS.

QUESTION: In 1936 Lawrence & Wishart published a slim volume entitled *Poems of Strife* by Julius Lipton. The poet was 24 years old; his book appeared in a limited edition of 95 copies. Library catalogues reveal that this was Lipton's only publication. Whatever happened to him?

☐ THANK YOU for your interest in my book, *Poems Of Strife*, which had an introduction by C. Day Lewis. The signed hardback was sold for five shillings, and a paperback edition of 1,000 followed, which sold at one shilling. A copy of the hardback can be seen at the magnificent Poetry Library in the Royal Festival Hall. I have not entirely disappeared, having been involved in theatre work and poetry publishing, and I am indexed in various publications. At 80, I am now engaged on a novel; the first 45,000 words have finally satisfied me, but my word processor will have to work a lot harder to at least double that number. Should it ever get published I will gladly send the questioner a copy.
Julius Lipton, Beckenham, Kent.

QUESTION: 'There's an old mill by the stream, Nellie Dean.' Who was Nellie Dean?

☐I DON'T think there was ever a real Nellie Dean. The song was made popular by a lady (stage name Gertie Gitana) who entertained the wounded soldiers of the First World War. My husband was one of them. Gertie Gitana is buried in the cemetery of the small town of Wigstan Magna, near Leicester. She died quite young and still pretty. Her husband put a magnificent white marble stone on her grave, and on it was engraved: 'There's an Old Mill by the Stream, Nellie Dean.' *(Mrs) L. Langland, Nottingham.*

QUESTION: The letters 'MC' seem to appear in almost every rap track and in the name of almost every rap group. What do they mean?

☐ MC stands for Master of Ceremonies. Ten to 15 years ago an MC's job was to introduce bands in clubs in the States. As several bands used to play in one night, competition was fierce and the MCs had to hype the bands as much as possible. The audiences were so impressed at their impromptu, rhyming, rhythmic rantings ('rapping') that these people became stars in their own right. *Alison Bray, Blagdon, Bristol.*

☐ BOTH MC and 'Toaster' clearly have their origins in the toastmaster/master of ceremonies who presides at banquets in white bourgeois society and so the terms may contain an element of critical parody. *Tim Wall, Prestwich, Manchester.*

☐ THE EQUINOX between the parallels of funk master beat and junk Jack master Jam is the area where in laybeat parlance the junk jive funk master cuts a cool beat to ensure the rap remains the same. The MC is the DJ who cuts a cool

groove in the rhythm machine and is the crucial cool Master Cutter aka the MC.
Nikki Walker featuring the crucial MC Clark, Windsor, Berks.

☐ THE letters MC stand for Microphone Controller, i.e. the person who actually does the rapping rather than the DJ (Disc Jockey) who plays, mixes and scratches the backing music.
Jonathan Walford, Media Research and Information Bureau, London.

QUESTION: Where can one buy an hourglass?

☐ FROM me: I make them, though not necessarily an exact hour.
Tony Barton, Madgeon Farm, Buckland St Mary, Chard, Somerset TA20 3QF. Tel: 046 034 213.

☐ I AM a woodturner and regularly make hourglasses of different woods, the most traditional being yew which in times past was used for Parsons glasses.
Robert T. Marwood, 95 Barn Meads Road, Wellington, Somerset TA21 9BD. Tel: 0823 667404

QUESTION: Why is an ice-cream cornet with chocolate flake known as a 99?

☐ IN 1930/31 my grandparents, William Henry and Laura Michael, took over a sweetshop at 99 London Road, Stockton Heath, Warrington. They stayed there until 1935. They started to make their own ice-cream, and I can remember an electric motor bolted to the red tiles on the floor and an ice chest in the yard. They served wafers and cornets, and scoops of ice-cream in customers' cups and glasses. Then they started to serve cornets with a Cadbury's Milk Flake pushed down into the ice-cream in the cornet, and I believe that was the origin of the 99-er. The fresh milk for the ice-cream was supplied by Claude Hughes of Grappenhall Road, Stockton Heath, in milk churns carried by horse and trap. Just before Claude died in 1969/70, I lent him a small album of photographs showing him delivering to the shop, and I never got them back.

Enid Spilsbury (née Michael), Stockton Heath, Warrington.

□ THE designation of 99 applies specifically to Cadbury's Chocolate Flake and its origins go back to the 1920s when Cadbury sales managers were actively cooperating with Italian ice cream manufacturers in the North-East and Scotland to enhance their products. Cadbury's Flake was first included in ice-cream sandwich wafers. It needed to be specially produced to the appropriate size. Later the cornet with the flake placed temptingly on top became the typical presentation. There are alternative explanations for the term '99' which run in company folklore: (1) In the days of the monarchy in Italy the king had a specially chosen guard consisting of 99 men, and subsequently anything really special or first class was known as '99'. (2) The name originated from the game housey-housey (now called bingo). The caller would refer to certain numbers with a form of slang. 'Clickety click' was 66 and 'top of the house' was 99.

R. B. Shaw, Cadbury Ltd, Bournville, Birmingham.

QUESTION: Who was St Pancras?

□ LITTLE is known about St Pancras other than his martyr-dom. *The Oxford Dictionary of Saints* lists two saints of the name. St Pancras of Taormina is reputed to have been sent by St Peter to evangelise Sicily, suffering martyrdom by stoning. St Pancras of Rome appears to have been a young nobleman from Phrygia (in modern Turkey) who suffered martyrdom at the age of 14 in Rome under the Emperor Diocletian, circa AD 304, for his adherence to the Christian faith. Veneration of St Pancras of Rome became popular in England after St Augustine made him the dedicatee of a church in Canterbury. The St Pancras area of London is named after a church dedicated to him: Old St Pancras in St Pancras Road, NW1, subsequently replaced by St Pancras church in Euston Square, an imposing Greek Revival building inspired by the Erechtheum in Athens. To most people the St Pancras area is best known for the railway station. Future generations may associate it with the new British Library under construction to the west of the station which opens in 1993.

Bart Smith, Press Officer, The British Library, London W1.

QUESTION: What are the true capabilities of TV detector vans?

□ IT IS easy to detect the magnetic field radiated from the deflection coils of the picture tube at a frequency of around 15kHz. With sensitive instruments it is possible to detect emissions from the set, and from its aerial, due to the local oscillator used to demodulate the incoming signal. In this way it is possible to distinguish the TV channel being watched and to distinguish TV channels from a video recorder, or computer equipment. However the true capability of the vans lies in their ability to 'remind' you to get a licence. The simplest method of detecting an unlicensed TV is to listen at the front window. It is also possible to detect local oscillator radiation from a radio. This had been used by MI5 (see, for example, *Spycatcher*) to detect when a radio receiver is tuned to a particular station. The radiation from the VDU and keyboard of a computer can be picked up on a short wave radio and decoded to display the data from the computer screen. All these emissions can be screened

against, but the cost of effective screening, including metal shields and aerial filters, is probably more than that of a licence.
David Gibson, Leeds.

☐ THE DETECTOR vans operated by the TV licensing arm of the Post Office can pinpoint a set in use at a range of up to 35 metres. They can determine the position of a set to within two feet and the programme being watched. To make evasion even more difficult, TV Licensing has brought into use hand-held detectors which can penetrate areas such as blocks of flats and pedestrian housing estates where detector vans are less convenient to operate.
Brian Hickman, Public Relations Department, The Post Office, London EC1.

☐ I CHALLENGE any reader to report having been caught by a detector van. The whole idea is a monstrous hoax perpetrated by propagandists such as Mr Hickman. The authorities identify licence-dodgers in much more mundane ways: when you buy or rent a TV, that fact is reported. Records are compared. They write to you and threaten you. *In extremis* they knock on your door.
R. M. Stewart, Caterham, Surrey.

☐ I CAN confirm what Mr Stewart says. Approximately annually I get either a form or a visit from the TV Licensing Authority to inquire why they have no record of a TV licence at my address. I then patiently explain approximately annually that it might be connected with the fact that I am one of that eccentric 1 per cent of the population who refuse to have a television.
Terry Richter, Fareham, Hants.

QUESTION: Is Britain the only country that considers it unnecessary to identify itself by name on its postage stamps?

☐ YES, and the reason is that Britain, in the person of Rowland Hill, invented the modern postal system, in honour of which the International Postal Organisation allows Britain, in this respect, to be unique.
Bernard ('Know-all') Levin, London W1.

☐ THE sovereign's head must appear on all stamps, including pictorials. On franked mail, where the portrait does not appear, the words 'Great Britain' must be printed.
Robert Tribe, Hassocks, Sussex.

QUESTION: Is there any impediment in civil or canon law to prevent the dead being buried in a vertical rather than horizontal position?

☐ NOT too far from here there is indeed a famous vertical burial (upside down into the bargain). Major Peter Labilliere was a very eccentric 18th-century gentleman who lived in Surrey. When he died, he left instructions that his landlady's son and daughter should dance on his coffin (alas, I don't know why) and when the dancing was through, he was to be buried head down vertically on Box Hill. This was done and a stone still marks the spot, right in the middle of a well-used footpath across the hill.
Hugh Lamb, Sutton, Surrey.

☐ IN THOSE societies which practise simple interment as the means of disposal of the dead, burial of the body in a flat grave has been the most common custom. Even where the body is inhumed horizontally wide variations are known with regard to orientation and disposition of the corpse, which may be supine, prone or lying on its side, and will be lying either fully extended or with its limbs drawn up. Important exceptions to horizontal burial have always been known. For example, in the Inca-dominated parts of South America the embalmed dead frequently were buried in a crouching posture, and among Australian aboriginal tribes some form of upright burial occasionally has been practised. Within the Christian tradition, burial technology has been dictated by a belief in the literal resurrection of the body. Thus, the faithful are buried oriented with feet to the East, the head facing the final dawn and straining to hear the last trump. Even here, however, exceptions are known, for, in certain arid parts of the world (Mexico, southern France and Spain, Sicily), some churches and catacombs display exhumed naturally mummified bodies in the vertical position (and not necessarily facing East). That vertical inhumation is not more prevalent is probably a consequence of practical and aesthetic considerations, rather than any prohibition upon the practice. Unless expertly and expensively embalmed, a dead body will disintegrate. While remaining undisturbed in a horizontal attitude the component bones will approximate to the human form. However, a vertically buried cadaver under gravity would deposit a jumble of disarticulated bones that might be regarded as unacceptable.

Bill White, Chesham, Bucks.

QUESTION: I have a wooden puzzle box, made in 1920-30, embossed 'Produced in aid of the Fresh Air Fund'. What was the Fresh Air Fund?

☐ IT WAS actually 'Pearson's Fresh Air Fund', founded in 1892 by the proprietors of *Pearson's Weekly*. A few years ago we changed its name to Pearson's Holiday Fund, as we began to receive strange telephone calls such as 'can you suggest a spray for my bathroom?' For nearly 100 years 'Pearson's' has been instrumental in sending thousands of

needy children from the large 'inner-city' conurbations tothe seaside and countryside. Almost all its limited income goes on this caring work, and will continue to do so, now that the social services have had their resources cut. *Pearson's Weekly* was later published by Newnes and then by IPC, but it foundered some years ago.
R. E. Heasman, Council Member, Pearson's Holiday Fund, London SW20.

□ THE HERALD Tribune Fresh Air Fund was a New York charity operating between the world wars. Financed by contributions, it sent needy city children on fortnight summer holidays to ordinary country families, who were paid 50 cents a day for each child. I don't know what happened to it, but have a vague memory of it functioning in the early 1950s.
Jessica Skippon, London WC2.

QUESTION: Warts, removal of. What do the old wives say?

□ I CAN'T vouch for old wives, but as a middle-aged blacksmith I regularly dispense bottles of 'bosh water' to children with warts, who just as regularly appear later with cleared hands. The bosh is the trough beneath the fire where the tongs are quenched, so it must contain some iron oxide among other additives. The instructions are: wash the hands last thing at night, apply the bosh water and let it dry on; after three months the warts will have disappeared. It really works.
P. J. Oberon, Middlesbrough, Cleveland.

□ OLD WIVES' tales are legion, and include rubbing with the

'milk' from a newly-picked dandelion flower; rubbing with the slime of the largest snail on the garden wall; covering with a piece of banana or onion skin; rubbing with a piece of raw meat, which is then buried at the crossroads by the light of the full moon; buying a wart from the sufferer for sixpence; strangling it with a hair plucked from a horse's tail, and many others. My own wart on my finger cleared after I had rubbed it well with the ink from my very first ballpoint pen, in about 1945. Hypnotism has been known to work with multiple warts, though as warts are said to be caused by a virus, all these seem odd. A far more sensible and certain removal is obtained by a visit to a State Registered Chiropodist, who may destroy it with various acids, or possibly remove it, painlessly, in one treatment, under local anaesthetic.

Brian L. Berry (BEd DPodM MChs), Society of Chiropodists, London W1.

QUESTION: What is the origin of the rather idiosyncratic names of some types of biscuits, such as Garibaldi?

☐ GARIBALDI biscuits were invented by Huntley & Palmer in 1864 and put on the market in that year when Giuseppe Garibaldi visited this country. He received an ecstatic welcome, as is described in chapter 21 of my book, *The Lion of Caprera*, and the whole country, apart from Queen Victoria and Karl Marx, rose to greet him. Incidentally, while I was correcting the proofs of my book in the sun outside a hotel in Spain a teacher from an American school asked me what I was doing. I told her I had just written a new biography of Garibaldi. There was a silence until she said brightly, 'Oh yes, the biscuit manufacturer'.

John Parris, Abingdon, Oxon.

QUESTION: Some pubs serving real ale refuse to provide vinegar with their bar meals. I am told it is because the vinegar can infect the beer, but how does this happen?

☐ VINEGAR is a dilute solution of acetic acid which is obtained by fermenting wine or 'wash' (a malt infusion). The most efficient way of doing this is by using a living fungus, the *Mycoderma aceti,* which flourishes in dilute alcoholic solutions and produces an enzyme, or complex organic catalyst, which brings about the reaction of alcohol (C_2H_5OH) and oxygen (O_2) to produce acetic acid (CH_3COOH) and water (H_2O). Real vinegar therefore still contains the fungus, which, one presumes, may be transferred to your favourite pint by spillage or travel through the air, and may then set to work souring your beer. If your landlord still refuses to provide vinegar with meals, politely suggest he gets some non-brewed condiment, which won't turn your beer into something so hideously unpalatable that it resembles lager.
Peter Finan, Eccleshill, Bradford.

QUESTION: At Christ Church Cathedral, Oxford, 'by long custom, Cathedral time is five minutes later than standard time.' Why?

☐ MY FRIEND at the cathedral told me it is to do with the coming of the railways. Accurate national timetabling required the synchronisation across the country of the previously-different regional times to coincide with the time at Greenwich. The canons of Christ Church, taking the long view, felt that standard national (and later, world) time was a new idea yet to prove its worth, and immediate action to fall in with the rest of the country would be premature. The ensuing decades have not altered their opinion but I am sure that the situation is kept under regular review.
Ian Pennell, Woodstock, Oxon.

☐ EVEN as late as 1841 the Great Western Railway were still having to advise on their timetables that 'London time is 4 min earlier than Reading time, 7½ min before Cirencester time and 14 min before Bridgwater time.' Consequently one can see that in this westerly gradation Oxford time would be about 5 minutes before a Greenwich 'standard' time. Most towns and villages quickly adapted to standardisation. Oxford and Christ Church Cathedral (happily) still do not conform

David Walsh, Guisborough.

QUESTION: A recently-published map of the Roman world shows in a dotted line a voyage St Paul is thought to have made to Spain. What is the evidence for this?

☐ THE EVIDENCE for St Paul's conjectural journey to Spain is firstly the hope expressed by him in Romans ch 15, vv 24 and 28 that he might travel as planned from Jerusalem to Rome and then on to Spain, and secondly the evidence provided by complete silence as to whether he carried out the final stage of these plans. The narrative of the Acts of the Apostles, which charts his other journeys and the shipwreck on the way to Rome, finishes on a high note of Paul's preaching unhindered in the capital of the Roman Empire. (Acts ch 28, v 30ff). It remains possible that he was able to travel in the western Mediterranean before his (traditional) martyrdom in Rome at the time of Nero. But the New Testament does not tell us, and later writers (1 Clement, the Muratorian Canon, and the Acts of Peter) seem to have more hard evidence than we do. If the Pastoral Epistles are late but authentic writings of Paul, they might suggest a further stage of journeying in the eastern Mediterranean, after the end of Acts (2 Timothy 4).

(Dr) J. M. Court, University of Kent, Canterbury.

QUESTION: Which was the first film to have a pre-credit sequence, and which film has the longest pre-credit sequence?

☐ THE FIRST film to have a pre-credit sequence was the 1934 melodrama, *Crime Without Passion*, directed by Ben Hecht and Charles MacArthur. It had an opening sequence designed by Slavko Vorkopitch, which begins with a shot of a gun being fired and blood dripping to the floor. From the blood the 'three Furies' (of Greek mythology) emerge and fly over a city, causing numerous crimes of passion. When one of the Furies sweeps her arm over the face of a skyscraper, the glass shatters and forms the title words of the film. The longest pre-title sequence is in the 1971 film, *The Last Movie*. The sequence actually lasts for 30 minutes, but then it was directed by that notable pretentious weirdo, Dennis Hopper.
Alan Dirrent, Poole, Dorset

☐ THE *Guinness Book of Film Facts and Feats* (Second Edition) states that the earliest pre-credit sequence is to be found in *Destry Rides Again* (1939), and that the longest is the half-hour which precedes the titles in *The Last Movie* (1971) While I have no quarrel with the former assertion, I believe the latter to be mistaken, for *Around the World in Eighty Days, Head, Woodstock* and *Apocalypse Now* have not only their credits at the end of the film (not uncommon practice) but also their very titles, turning, in effect, the whole film into one long pre-credit sequence. Therefore, *Woodstock*, with a running time of 184 minutes, should be considered the film with the longest pre-credit sequence.
Julian Morruzi, Caerphilly, Mid-Glamorgan

QUESTION: Popular tradition has it that the last words of William Pitt (the younger) were: I think I could eat one of Bellamy's veal pies'. Who was Bellamy?

☐ WILLIAM Pitt the Younger was, towards the end of his life,

owing to financial improvidence, forced to sell his home and was living in a rented house in Richmond opposite the Grand Lodge of Lord Addington. Edward Bellamy was a grocer whose shop was on Putney High Street, not far from the junction with Upper Richmond Road. He was a noted supplier of delicacies to the gentry of the area and doubtless therefore supplied veal pies to the Pitt household. Bellamy had nine children and the second son emigrated to America where by repute he founded the family of which Edward Bellamy, the noted novelist and historian, was a member. (I have not, in fact, been able to secure documentary evidence of this point.)
Ann Franklin, Milton Keynes.

☐ '[JOHN] Bellamy had been appointed Deputy House-keeper in the Palace of Westminster in 1773. He was persuaded to provide food on the premises, and did so with evident success. Bellamys, father and son, fed the Commons until 1834 when their kitchen was gutted in the fire.' From: *Inside the House of Commons*, by John Biffen MP, 1989, p. 180.
Rob Shepherd, London SW10.

QUESTION: Why do we kiss?

☐ BEN Whitaker in his book, *The Global Fix*, states that kissing is merely a way for lovers to test each other's semiochemicals. These are chemical substances that communicate biological signals between animals and which are produced by the sebaceous glands. Falling in love may only be a 'high' caused by addiction to another person's semiochemicals. Fortunately these drugs are not restricted under the Misuse of Drugs Act 1971.
Gill Kwik, National Drugs Intelligence Unit, New Scotland Yard, London SW1.

QUESTION: Why is glass transparent?

☐ GLASS is a material which has formed by cooling from the liquid state and has not crystallised, but remained amorphous. It is in effect a rigid liquid. It is transparent because structurally it is a large molecule containing no internal surfaces, holes or inclusions that have any dimensions approaching the wavelength of light. Light may therefore pass through unhindered.

K. E. Parker/D. T. Evans, Thorn Lighting Ltd, Leicester.

☐ 'ORDINARY' glass is opaque at short wavelengths (less than 300 nanometres) and also at long wavelengths (greater than 4,000 nanometres). We can see a band of wavelengths in between – 350 to 750 nanometres – where most glasses are intrinsically transparent. The absorption which causes opacity at short wavelengths involves electrons in the ions which make up the glass being activated by the light to higher energy levels. The necessary energy is taken from the light beam. The absorption at long wavelengths is taken up by the ions in the glass vibrating with greater amplitude. Because of the nature of the ions in ordinary glass and the way they are bonded together, neither of these mechanisms is active to any great extent in the range of visible wavelengths. It is easy to make coloured and even black glass by adding to the melt ions such as cobalt, manganese, nickel, etc, which absorb light by the electron excitation mechanism. Conversely making glass very transparent for optical communication fibres requires the complete elimination of these colouring elements. Some glasses are intrinsically opaque, e.g. those made by the extremely rapid cooling of certain alloys. Though it may seem unlikely, these glasses have valuable technical applications.

H. Rawson, Emeritus Professor of Glass Technology, University of Sheffield.

☐ A MATERIAL is transparent when an object can be seen clearly through it. This requires several things. First the surfaces of the material must be smooth and shiny so that light rays are transmitted in a regular way. Glasses are cooled from the liquid state without important change in most of their properties and naturally have the mirror-like surface of a liquid; if this has been impaired they can be polished. A rough surface scatters the light and spoils transparency as occurs with ground or frosted glass or snow. Second, there must be little loss of light by reflection at the surface. There is some reflection loss whenever light crosses from one medium into another but this is small for glasses; a loss of about 8 per cent is typical for a sheet of glass. Reflection loss can be made almost zero by applying special coatings, as is often done with camera lenses, or may be made almost complete by other coatings (e.g. silver) to make a mirror. Third, the internal structure of the material must not scatter the light. Glasses lack internal boundaries at which light rays could be scattered or reflected and have the same random arrangement of atoms in all directions so that light rays pass through in exactly the same way in all directions; glasses therefore give no image distortion on this account. Fourth, the material must not appreciably absorb the light. Light travels as packets of energy which vibrate at different rates, the rate of vibration determining its colour. If any parts of the atoms in the material can vibrate at the same rate as the light its energy is trapped inside the material and the light is absorbed; none or very little may then be transmitted to form an image. The kinds of atoms which make up common glasses do not vibrate at the same rates as visible light and the light is not absorbed. By changing the composition of the glass it can be made to absorb some of the visible spectrum, which produces a coloured glass, or all of the visible range which makes a black glass. Glasses can be made to absorb or transmit some of the ultra violet or infra red (heat) radiation whether or not they are transparent to visible light.

(Prof) Michael Cable, School of Materials, University of Sheffield.

QUESTION: Iz ther a sosaieti that beleevz thee Inglish langwidge shud bee spelt az it iz spoeken?

☐ IF THEE letus mi childrun bring hom frum thee lokul comprihensiv skool ar enithing tu go bi, ther iz indeed sutch a sosaieti — it iz corld thee Nashunl Yoonyun ov Teechus.
Yorz sinseerli, Jefri Klaak (Jeffrey Clarke), Macclesfield, Cheshire.

☐ THE answer is yes: there have been such societies since the 19th century. The main one today, based in the UK, but with links around the world, is the Simplified Spelling Society. While the SSS believes all alphabetic scripts are best designed so that pronunciation determines spelling, and spelling reflects pronunciation, this ideal cannot easily be applied to modern English. For one thing, English has no standard pronunciation on which to base such a spelling system; and for another, the changes required would be so radical as to produce an upheaval in world communication. However, many small improvements to English spelling could be easily introduced. We could get rid of 'gh'. We could write delt, hed, helth, mesure, etc. We could align the endings of burglar, teacher, doctor, neighbour, murmur, martyr, or of assistant, consistent, etc. We could tidy up such anomalies as speak/speech, high/height. We could all write 'acomodation' and 'comitee' — as many people already do. We could cut out innumerable redundant letters, making all writing faster. The Simplified Spelling Society would like to hear from all those interested in pursuing the question.
Christopher Upward, Membership Secretary, Simplified Spelling Society, 61 Valentine Road, Birmingham B14 7AJ.

☐ ILLOGICALITY is one of the few good attributes of the English and should not be tampered with.
Helen McGinty, Blackpool, Lancs.

☐ THE PROBLEM would be, spoken by whom? In different parts of England I have heard the word 'come' pronounced variously as kum, koom, kim and kahm.

(Mrs) Janet Money, Maryport, Cumbria.

☐ I BILEEVD in funetik speling until Ie bot dhu Sho Alfubet Eedishun uv Andruklaes und dhu Lieun. Whie wer dhaer difurunt voulz in kat und fadhur, in good und food? Hou kood Ie get foer spelings for to, tor, toer, und toor? Dhu problum iz dhut eedhur speling must vaeri from reejun to reejun, from klas to klas, or wee ol have tu aksept dhee arbitruri speling uv wun groop. Gleskurantu rrolz OK?

Yoorz faethfuli, Arnold Edward, Cheltenham, Glos.

☐ THE following quotation might offer a possible solution: A Plan for the Improvement of English Spelling by Mark Twain. For example, in Year 1 that useless letter 'c' would be dropped to be replased either by 'k' or 's', and likewise 'x' would no longer be part of the alphabet. The only kase in which 'c' would be retained would be the 'ch' formation, which will be dealt with later. Year 2 might reform 'w' spelling, so that 'which' and 'one' would take the same konsonant, wile Year 3 might well abolish 'y' replasing it with 'i' and Iear 4 might fiks the 'g/j' anomali wonse and for all. Jenerally, then, the improvement would kontinue iear bai iear with Iear 5 doing awai with useless double konsonants, and Iears 6-12 or so modifaiing vowlz and the rimeining voist and unvoist konsonants. Bai Iear 15 or sou, it wud fainali bi posibl tu meik ius ov thi ridandant letez 'c', 'y' doderez – tu riplais 'ch', 'sh', and 'th' rispektivli. Fainali, xen, aafte sam 20 iers ov orxogrefkl riform, wi wud hev a lojikl, kohirnt speling in ius xrewawt xe Ingliy-spiking werld.

David Tong, Manchester.

QUESTION: Does anybody know the origin of the hammer and sickle as a political symbol? I was once informed by a work colleague that it originated among Russian exiles in America, but I have never been able to prove or refute this theory.

☐ THIS clearly symbolises the rule of the proletariat, industrial and rural. But it may well be an adaptation of a much older Russian symbol: that of the cross above the upturned crescent, celebrating the triumph of Christianity over Islam. This can still be seen crowning one of the domes of St Basil's cathedral in Moscow.
D. R. Howison, Oakham, Rutland.

☐ D. R. HOWISON is wrong on two counts. The sickle represents not the 'rural proletariat' but the peasantry. 'Rural proletarians' are wage labourers with no direct interest in the land they farm, and only a tiny fraction of the rural population in pre-revolutionary Russia. This may seem a quibble, but it was a vital factor in Lenin's revolutionary strategy. Nor is the hammer-and-sickle emblem based (other than perhaps unconsciously) on the crescent surmounted by the cross. The Bolsheviks would have had no desire to elevate the Orthodox Church above Islam, and in any case the Communist emblem would require a 45-degree rotation to bear even a passing resemblance to the anti-Islamic one. The hammer and sickle was in fact a simplified development of the earlier emblem of the Russian Social-Democratic Labour Party (Bolsheviks) which appeared on the 1918 propaganda poster, 'Denikin's Band', as the hammer crossed with the plough. This emblem also appeared within the red star of the earliest cap badges of the Red Army. Unfortunately I cannot name its originator, or say whether it was ever an official state emblem. By the time of the founding of the USSR, it had been completely replaced by the simpler and more easily recognised hammer and sickle.

Denver Walker, Bristol.

□ THE ORIGINS are obscure, but according to Stephen White, an authority on Bolshevik iconography, the famous symbol of unity between workers and peasants first made its appearance in Saratov in 1917 as the emblem of the local Soviet. It swiftly became popular and by July 1918 the first Soviet constitution adopted it as the state symbol of the RSFSR.

John Gorman, Waltham Abbey, Essex.

HE'S TRYING TO FORGET.

QUESTION: Do elephants really have such good memories?

□ THE ORIGIN of the belief that elephants have long memories comes from the works of 'Saki' (H. H. Munro), 1870–1916. In his book, *Reginald On Besetting Sins*

(1910), he wrote: 'Women and elephants never forget an injury.' Readers will be able to judge for themselves whether this is likely to be true of elephants from their personal knowledge as to whether it is true about women.
A. J. G. Glossop, Pwllheli, Gwynedd.

☐ THE BELIEF that elephants have good memories is older than Saki's epigram; in fact it has an ancient lineage. Plutarch (1st century AD) repeats a story of Hagnon of Tarsus (2nd century BC) about an elephant whose keeper daily defrauded it of half its provender. One day, however, as the owner looked on, the servant poured out the full measure of grain. The clever Nelly seeing this, divided the grain into two heaps, thereby exposing the cheat. The belief is also common in stories from Mughal India, while Edward Topsell in *The Historie of Foure-Footed Beasts* (1607) wrote: 'when they are hurt by any man, they seldom forget a revenge.' Elephants, like Androcles' lion, are also said to remember acts of kindness; although, sadly, these are not so many as injuries.
Stuart McLaren, Norwich, Norfolk.

☐ COLONEL W Williams, known as 'Elephant Bill', once gave a talk in Imphal in the forward area of the Burma Front to a large audience of members of the 14th Army. One of his stories was of an elephant with a huge abscess on his back, which Bill had to lance with a Burmese Dah. Each evening the wound was washed and dressed by Bill at sundown. When the wound healed, the 'patient' went to work in a different area for some years. By chance this animal and Bill came together again and the elephant came to his bungalow at sundown and knelt down to show the scar (or get treatment). He certainly remembered the place and the man.
Ken Llewellyn (ex-23rd Army Air Support Control), Cardiff.

QUESTION: Inspired by the review of the film, *Lord Of The Flies* (William Golding), I would be interested to identify the author of a probably Victorian or Edwardian short story entitled 'King Of The Flies' having as its central character a boy possessed by evil.

□ THE STORY the questioner is referring to is almost certainly 'The Idol Of The Flies' by Jane Rice. It tells of Pruitt, one of the most monstrous children in literature, who progresses from torturing insects to murder, and eventually attracts the attention of Asmodeus. This demonic figure despatches Pruitt in a cloud of flies in one of the most satisfying ends to a story you could wish to find. Far from being Victorian or Edwardian, it first appeared in the magazine, *Unknown Worlds*, in 1942, and has been reprinted often since then. It would be interesting to ascertain if William Golding ever read it. As a subject for gruesome stories, flies are not that common. Jane Rice's story is one of the best of that small bunch.
Hugh Lamb, Sutton, Surrey.

QUESTION: Can anyone give a reasonable explanation as to why approval should be indicated by clapping the hands together?

□ I SUGGEST that hand clapping is a spontaneous and unconscious gesture of joy in young children attempting to grasp an object of delight with both hands copied by an adult more or less consciously as a trick of flattery.
M. Fuggle, Huddersfield.

□ ONE of the first signs of conscious pleasure in a baby is the banging of its hands together when it sees a known and loved person approaching. It is thought by believers in evolution that this has developed from the apes and gorillas who also do this.
(Mrs) N. F. Gould, Guildford, Surrey.

QUESTION: Why are there so many Coldharbour Lanes? What does the name mean?

☐ THE VICTORIAN author, Isaac Taylor, in *Words And Places*, first published 1864, states: 'The ruins of deserted Roman villas were no doubt often used (as overnight shelter) by travellers who carried their own bedding and provisions, as is done by the frequenters of the khans and dak houses of the East. Such places seem commonly to have borne the name of Cold Harbour. Near ancient lines of road we find no less than 70 places bearing this name, and about a dozen more bearing the analogous name of Caldicot, or "cold cot".' He compares the word 'harbour' with the German *herberg* and the French *auberge* meaning 'shelter'. In support of this, the Coldharbour Lane in Brixton is close to the Roman road running through Streatham (the 'dwelling' on the 'paved road', or 'street'); and Coldharbour village near Dorking, Surrey is close to Stane Street (the 'paved road'). Readers living near Akeman Street, Ermine Street, Icknield Street, the Portways and Fosse Way will find other examples. It would be interesting to know whether other 'coldharbours' exist which do not lie near Roman roads or villas. In the Dark Ages, in the Anglo Saxon period and the Middle Ages, a domestic traveller on foot would travel perhaps 10 to 15 miles a day. Although there were many hostels run by the religious houses for travellers, a 'cold harbour' was probably preferable to sleeping rough, when a hostel was not available.

Anne Andrews, Reigate.

☐ FRANCIS Brett Young, in his novel, *Cold Harbour*, says the name is derived from the Latin, *colonia arborum*, a grove.

H. Webster, Brixham, Devon.

QUESTION: Who was the curate whose egg was 'good in parts'?

☐ THE HAPLESS curate is misquoted as often as he is misunderstood. In a *Punch* cartoon of 1895, a bishop, eating breakfast with a fresh-faced curate, says: 'I'm afraid you've got a bad egg, Mr Jones!' To which the curate replies: 'Oh no, my Lord, I assure you. Parts of it are excellent!' The phrase is mainly used (I contend wrongly) to describe a mixed blessing. Eggs, of course, are either good or bad. So the curate may be (a) romantic, seeing good in all things; (b) sycophantic, aiming to please his boss; (c) unrealistic, blind to the facts; (d) an unashamed compromiser; (e) uncomplaining; or (f) strong-stomached. I favour (a).
Jeremy McMullen, London WC2.

QUESTION: I often leave work early so that I can watch the reruns of *The Lone Ranger* on Channel 4. Recently, to my horror, the Lone Ranger has been played by John Hart. What happened to Clayton Moore? Also, I have heard that 'Kimosabe', Tonto's term of endearment to his companion, was an Indian insult. Is this correct?

☐ THE short answer is that after the first series during 1949–50 Clayton Moore asked for more money to continue with the part. He was reported at the time as getting around $500 per episode. When this was refused he left the series and returned to working on movies. John Hart, who replaced him for the second series, was a good horseman but lacked acting experience. Moore returned for the third series in 1954 and remained until the series ended production in 1957. For the history of the Lone Ranger consult *Who Was That Masked Man?* by David Rothel.
James Scott, Muirend, Glasgow.

☐ THE MEANING of Tonto's term of endearment to his

companion became clear in an episode broadcast on Channel 4 on December 19, 1989, where Tonto himself states that 'Kimosabe means trusty scout'. Incidentally, the question of the meaning of Kimosabe has vexed other minds apart from the questioner's. I remember the issue being raised (in passing) at an international conference on social psychology and language in 1979. Nobody knew the answer.
Brian M. Young, PhD, Department of Psychology, University of Exeter.

☐ KIMOSABE may well be an insult given that Tonto is the Spanish word for 'stupid'.
Carey Evans, Teddington, Middx.

☐ I'VE ALWAYS understood Kimosabe to be a corruption of the Spanish 'Quien no sabe' ('He who knows nothing'). Presumably this was Tonto's revenge.
Malcolm Jones, Stony Stratford, Bucks.

☐ IN THE mountains of Arizona, 50 miles east of Phoenix, is the Tonto National Monument: named not after the Lone Ranger's sidekick but the Tonto Apaches, one of the many subdivisions of the tribe whose names derive from the days when Arizona was part of Mexico. The Tonto Apaches, still to be found on the state's Indian reservations, were named after the Tonto river. The Apaches themselves, like many other tribes, prefer to call themselves simply 'the people' – Tinde in their language. Delshay, a contemporary of Geronimo (another Mexican name – he was known to his own people as Goyakhle, 'The Yawner'), was the last great chief of the Tonto Apaches. He was murdered by bounty hunters of his own tribe in 1874 and had his head displayed thereafter on a US Army parade ground. It would never make a TV series.
L. Raphael, Kilmaurs, Strathclyde.

QUESTION: Was Winston Churchill the first person to use the two-fingered V-for-Victory sign?

☐ DURING the blitz the BBC's European Intelligence Director, Jonathan Griffin, told his boss, John Lawrence, the European Services Organiser, that his postbag from Europe indicated a need for a visual symbol of resistance and liberation. Towards the end of 1940, after a bout of flu, Lawrence found on the agenda of his Belgian Committee at Bush House an item to be discussed: the V-sign. The first public mention of the V-sign was in a broadcast on January 14, 1941, by the Belgian Programme Organisers, Victor de Laveleye. The feedback from Belgium and elsewhere was such that a general campaign was launched, later to include the V-sound in morse (. . . –) and the opening bar of Beethoven's Fifth Symphony (. . . –). Churchill was publicly associated with the campaign for the first time in a broadcast message on July 18 or 19. But in the opinion of Lawrence, the germ of the idea was Griffin's. After discussion on the Belgian Committee, de Laveleye gave the idea its shape and rationale: V was the initial letter of Victory, not only in English but also in French/Walloon and Flemish, and easily scribbled on walls in the dark. More details can be found in Asa Briggs' *History of the BBC* and in C. J. Rolo's *Radio Goes To War* (1943). Incidentally, I have heard that later in the war Churchill – to the delight of the troops – would make the V-for-Victory sign and immediately convert it into the sweeping gesture telling Hitler to – – – – off. Can any eye-witness confirm this?
Anthony Rudolf, London N12.

☐ CHURCHILL wasn't the first to use it, by a long way. Before the battle of Agincourt, the greatest fear among the French was of the formidable English bowmen. In an effort to defuse the threat of the 15th-century version of the cruise missile, the night before the battle they called across the lines, warning the English that any bowman captured the

next day would have his first two fingers – those used to draw back the bowstring – lopped off. At first light, the English archers assembled in sight of the French lines, brandishing threatened, now threatening, digits in a gesture which has since been used by Churchill in a similar spirit, but also by Harvey Smith and numerous footballers and cricketers in a spirit much closer to the original.
Mark Power, Bristol.

QUESTION: What is 'swashbuckling', and how do you do it?

☐ YOU swash, or rattle, your buckler (small round shield) with your sword, in order to make a lot of noise and frighten the enemy.
Peter Mellor, City University, London.

☐ SWASHBUCKLING is still practised by riot police in this country and elsewhere when they drum on their shields with their batons.
Anthony Jackson, Felpham.

QUESTION: Who was Bobby Shafto and what was the buckle on his knee?

☐ THE words of Bobby Shafto were first written down in 1805 and more than likely are a shortened version of the original which lampooned the career of one Robert Shafto (1732–1797) of Whitworth Hall. He was a shipowner who had offices at Newcastle docks and only occasionally went to sea. From his portrait it would appear that he was quite striking in appearance. He was engaged to a Miss Bellasis, a rich heiress of Brancepeth who it is said died of a broken heart when he broke off the engagement. He married Anne Duncombe from Duncombe Park, Yorkshire, and, according to legend, managed to squander most of her money. He represented Durham in Parliament from 1760 to 1768 and afterwards represented the borough of Downtown, Wiltshire. The rhyme was more than likely penned by political rivals and the tune is an adaptation of an old Northumbrian ditty, 'Willy Foster's gone to sea . . . Canny Willy Foster', mentioned by Sir Walter Scott in *Redgauntlet* (1824). The second and third verses describe him as fat and fair' and appealing to ladies. The now unheard fourth and fifth verses celebrate Shafto's capacity to spend money while ignoring the needs of his electorate. The silver buckles at his knee mentioned in the first verse neatly underscore the original purpose of the rhyme.

John Bates, Harlech, Gwynedd

QUESTION: I saw in a film recently a fictional episode in which a diver discovered intact amphorae in the wreck of an ancient Greek ship. On breaking the seals he found the wine to be drinkable. Is this possible?

□ THE answer is no. The uses of amphorae for liquids dates the shipwreck to hundreds of years old. During that time any seal or stopper is quickly eaten away by crustacea and the properties of seawater. When the ship sinks, it settles with the amphorae invariably at the top, resting at an angle, neck upwards. It is the shape of these amphorae, covered with sediment, that indicates a wreck. When we bring them to the surface, they are thickly covered with rock-hard crustacea, but no liquids have ever been found in them. On the other hand, we once found off the coast of Italy an unopened crate of ancient Roman pottery, complete with the straw packing.

A. P. Pulleyn-Holden, Bishop's Castle, Shropshire.

QUESTION: Why do words beginning 'sl...' almost invariably have unpleasant meanings?

□ SHE WAS sloe-eyed, slender and slinky. She slipped into her slacks, slaked her thirst, and enjoyed a slap-up yet slimming meal. Then feeling sleek and slaphappy, she slept.
Cass Robertson, Cambridge.

□ ANALYSIS of the 76 words beginning with sl... in *Chambers Gem Dictionary* 1987, shows that four have pleasant meanings, 32 are neutral, and 40 have unpleasant meanings. Furthermore, slim can be pleasant if applied to a girl, but unpleasant if applied to your purse. There are effectively no words beginning with 'sl' in French or Spanish; and too few in Italian to draw any conclusions. Words in German beginning with the equivalent 'schl' appear to have roughly the same range as in English.
R. M. Nartill, Stockton-on-Tees, Cleveland.

QUESTION: Can anyone supply any information on a story which has been around for some time, that a beer manufacturer, on hearing that shanty town people in South America were using empty bottles as building bricks, produced batches of square-shaped bottles? This was possibly in Sao Paulo in the 1960s.

□ ALTHOUGH the use of glass bottles as a building material is as old as the bottle itself, and patents exist as far back as the early 1900s for attempts to design a combined bottle and brick, the first mass production container designed with the specific intention of secondary use as a building component was the WOBO (World Bottle) developed by Heineken in the 1960s. The project was initiated after a visit to the Caribbean Island of Curacao in 1960 by the brewery head, Alfred Heineken. Observing the poor living conditions of the population — shanty huts primarily constructed from seashore flotsam – and unsightly quantities of discarded beer bottles (although collection and re-use was the norm in Europe it was, as nowadays, economically unviable there, and in many exports markets), Heineken envisaged building use as a potential solution to both problems. John Habrakan, an innovative Dutch architect, was commissioned to work with in-house researchers to develop both the bottle and building system. This culminated in 1963 when 100,000 prototype WOBOs were produced, together with plans for a simple dwelling small enough to be printed on the label. The bottle was square in section with a short neck designed to fit into a recess on the bottom of its neighbour when laid horizontally. The sides were moulded with small, round projections which aided bonding with mortar. Although a prototype house was built near Amsterdam, Habraken's simple and low cost original plans were corrupted in an attempt to make the image of the building more acceptable to those who saw bottles as bottles and houses as houses and could not connect the two. Sixty thousand of the bricks were apparently still lying on a Rotterdam warehouse in the early 1970s. Can anyone say what happened next?

Chris James, Senior Lecturer, Department of Industrial Design, Coventry Polytechnic.

QUESTION: When was the skip invented, and by whom? Was it a product of inner-city gentrification?

☐ ALTHOUGH skips have been used in the mining industry for a long time, the first use of a skip-like container removed by a lorry for rubbish disposal was probably in Southport in 1922. The development came about as a result of Edwin Walker, of the lorry manufacturer Pagefield, meeting Southport's borough engineer. He, like other towns' engineers, faced the problem of growing distances between household refuse collection rounds and dumping grounds. Horse-drawn refuse carts were effective in town, but not in cover-

ing the distances to waste tips. The resulting Pagefield system used 300 cu ft horse-drawn containers on 20-inch diameter wheels which, when full, were winched on to the back of a Pagefield lorry to make a relatively speedy trip to a distant dump. A more up-to-date system, not relying on horses, but still created by municipal enterprise and needs and not by the purely commercial initiatives of modern-day skip hire operators, was launched by the Letchworth firm of S & D in 1926. Harry Shelvoke and his partner, James Drewry, had developed a revolutionary, small-wheeled petrol-engined truck – the Freighter – in 1922. It had hand control to make things easier for ex-horsemen to drive. Scores of applications followed, including in 1926 a system featuring sideways-mounted skips for the Marylebone area of London. Several skips could be carried across the chassis at once. The Freighter, with all its different applications, was such a good idea that it is time someone re-invented it. The present day skip is, environmentalists please note, less clean than those early Pagefield and S & D systems – they had closely-fitting lids on their containers. The growth of DIY as a leisure activity and the need to replace parts of Victorian houses (not just repair them) have probably contributed as much to skip growth as outright gentrification of our inner suburbs.
Stephen Jolly, Milton Keynes, Bedfordshire.

☐ ALTHOUGH the skip may have changed the face of gentrification, that process is older than the skip. I was taught about gentrification in A level geography in the 1960s, but first encountered skips in the early 1970s, working in a small engineering factory in Reading. The factory waste was thrown into a skip, supplied by a firm from Ewelme called Grundon. The command was always 'Put it in the grundon', and it was only much later that I discovered that this remarkably apt name was not the correct term. I still think of them as 'grundons'.
Rob Close, Ayr, Scotland.

QUESTION: Does anyone know the author and title of a poem in which a man on a train is trying to engage a fellow passenger in conversation, only to have all his questions answered by the word 'Quite'?

☐ THE word used in the poem is not quite 'quite' but 'quate'. The title is 'A Quate-So Story' by an unknown author. It is a cautionary tale, since the 'Youth who wore canary spats,/ The very latest thing in hats,/And on his cheeks two little mats/Of whisker (fluff, at any rate)', comes to a sticky end for infuriating the fellow passenger by answering every comment with Quate'. The poem concludes:

. . . I kicked and beat
The languid youth from head to feet
And stuffed him underneath the seat,
And then, in tones made hoarse with hate,
I thundered, 'Are you satisfied
That it was fully time you died?'
Bloodless of face and filmy-eyed
He whispered, 'Quate!'

Phil Gane, Ingatestone, Essex.

☐ THE poem can be found in an anthology entitled *Travelling Light* which was published by Oliver and Boyd in 1962.
G. E. Lightfoot, Ladybridge, Bolton.

☐ I discovered the poem in a wartime anthology, *Humour in Verse*, compiled by W. E. Slater (Cambridge University Press, 1943). It emanated from *Punch* according to the acknowledgements.
S. P. Taylor, New Milton, Hants.

QUESTION: What do the pyramid and the eye represent on the American $1 note?

☐ THE DEVICE on the note is the reverse side of the Great

Seal of the United States. The seal was adopted by Congress on June 20, 1782. Only the obverse was ever cut and put to use, although the design of the reverse still exists in theory. The symbols on both sides emerged after a long period of discussion, as analysed very ably in *The Eagle and the Shield* by Richard Patterson and Richardson Dougall (Department of State, Washington, 1976). The symbols on the reverse are an unfinished pyramid of 13 courses, an eye representing Providence, the date 1776 in Roman numerals and the mottoes: 'Annuit Coeptis' and 'Novus Ordo Seclorum'. The first is a phrase from Virgil and can be said to mean 'He favours our undertakings' – the 'he' being the deity represented by the eye. The second means 'A new order of the ages' and is also from Virgil. There is no doubt that the eye and the pyramid are Masonic in origin, and it seems likely that Francis Hopkinson, a Mason, was responsible for bringing these elements into the national emblems. The reverse of the seal was incorporated into the dollar bill by an act of President Roosevelt, dated July 2, 1935.

William G. Crampton, Director, The Flag Institute, Chester.

☐ THE EYE (or deity), in looking down on the pyramid, can see all of its sides equally (excluding the base) and as such is

a representation of democracy. At any other corner, the eye could only see two of its faces.
David Shakespeare, London SW8.

☐ IN KURT Vonnegut's book, *Breakfast of Champions*, the author writes: 'If they [the Americans] studied their paper money for clues as to what their country was all about, they found, among a lot of other Baroque trash, a picture of a truncated pyramid with a radiant eye on top of it. Not even the President of the United States knew what it was all about. It was as though the country were trying to say to its citizens, "IN NONSENSE IS STRENGTH".'
Daniel Jones, Northants.

☐ ROBERT Anton Wilson and Robert Shea, in their paranoid conspiracy novel *Illuminatus*, quote the story that the Great Seal was given to Benjamin Franklin by a masked stranger who appeared in Franklin's garden one evening. American friends tell me this story is well known. (In fact, when I was at college, a fellow student checked every single reference from *Illuminatus* in the university library, and found them all to be genuine.) The masonic origin of the symbol is hardly surprising, given the connection between freemasonry and Liberal politics in the 18th century.
Daniel Jacobs, London NW4.

QUESTION: What are the unsung anti-Scottish verses of the National Anthem?

☐ ACCORDING to Fitzroy MacLean's *A Concise History of Scotland*, the following additional verse to the National Anthem was sung in music halls in London at the time of the 1745 Jacobite rebellion:
> *God grant that Marshall Wade,*
> *May by Thy mighty aid*
> *Victory bring.*

> *May he sedition hush*
> *And like a torrent rush*
> *Rebellious Scots to crush*
> *God save the King.*

Presumably similar sentiments were expressed by anti-Jacobites in Scotland too. The official second verse of the (British) National Anthem which is generally unsung is a more general piece of invective:

> *Oh Lord our God arise,*
> *Scatter our enemies and make them fall*
> *Confound their politics,*
> *Frustrate their knavish tricks,*
> *On Thee our hopes we fix.*
> *God save us all!*

Grieg Rattay, Hatfield, Herts.

☐ IN THE existing second verse the politics to be frustrated and the knavish tricks to be confounded were those of the Jacobites. Another Jacobite version of 1760 runs:

> *God bless the happy hour:*
> *May the Almighty Power*
> *Make all things well;*
> *That the whole progeny*
> *Who are in Italy*
> *May soon and suddenly*
> *Come to Whitehall.*

Roy Palmer, Dymock, Glos.

☐ A LETTER to the *Times* on February 27, 1878, claimed that the origin of the tune and original words were in fact Scottish, and were:

> *God save the King, I pray*
> *God bless the King, I pray*
> *God save the King.*
> *Send him victorious*
> *Happy and glorious*
> *Soon to reign over us*

God save the King.
God bless the Prince of Wales
The true born Prince of Wales
Sent us by thee.
Grant us one favour more
The King for to restore
As thou hast done before
The Familie. Amen.

These words suggest origins earlier than 1715. Far more in depth information can be found in William Cummings' *God Save the King* (Novello). Also there are two interesting Scottish versions of the National Anthem on pages 50–53 of volume 2 of Hogg's *Relics*, published in 1819.

Jon Atkinson, Orchestral Librarian, BBC TV Music Library, London.

QUESTION: Can Aids be transmitted by mosquitoes, in the same way that they infect people with malaria in tropical countries?

□ THE QUESTION has been carefully considered by an expert panel and their conclusions, entitled, *Do Insects Transmit Aids?* published by the Office of Technology Assessment of the United States Congress (1987). Theoretically there are two ways in which biting insects or acarines might transmit HIV infections: by biological transmission or by mechanical transmission. Biological transmission is the kind of cycle known for malaria parasites and numerous truly insect-transmitted viruses (arboviruses), e.g. yellow fever virus. Whereas yellow fever virus grows in and can be transmitted by mosquitoes in the laboratory and grows in mosquito tissue cultures, experiments have failed to show any evidence that HIV can grow in various insects or insect or tick cell cultures. Certain viruses, e.g. Rift Valley Fever virus, can be mechanically transmitted without replication in the mosquito, i.e. when a feeding mosquito is disturbed, virus adhering to the mouthparts is carried to another person or animal on which the bloodmeal is completed. However, unlike Rift Valley Fever virus, the concentration of HIV in the blood is very low and calculations show an extremely small chance of mechanical transmission of an infectious dose. In Africa, where HIV infection and biting insects are very common, infection is virtually only seen in sexually active adults and in babies of infected women but rarely in children, whereas malaria and arbovirus infections are common in children. Thus there seems little possibility of insect transmission as a significant factor in the spread of Aids.

(Drs) Colin Leake and Christopher Curtis, School of Hygiene and Tropical Medicine, London WC1.

□ IF BLOOD-sucking insects did inject the blood obtained from one person in to another, they might transmit Aids and some other diseases. Fortunately for man they don't. If they inject anything when they bite it is a salivary secretion, usually through a separate channel in the mouthparts to the one taking in the blood. The saliva contains an anti-clotting agent to prevent blocking the tube through which the blood is obtained, and it is this secretion which causes some people to react after the bite. A mosquito obtains the malarial parasite in infected blood but inside the insect the parasite changes its form and must get into the mosquito's salivary glands to be injected into another person. There is no evidence that the Aids virus can get into the salivary glands. The situation appears to be similar for most of the piercing blood-suckers such as fleas, lice, bedbugs and ticks, and it is not thought that Aids (or hepatitis B) could be transmitted by their bite.

Sir James Beament, Queens' College, Cambridge.

QUESTION: Why is the Nine of Diamonds known as the Curse of Scotland?

☐ AFTER the Battle of Culloden, the order to hunt down the supporters of 'Bonnie Prince Charlie' was written on the back of a nine of diamonds playing card by the Duke of Cumberland – remembered since then as 'Butcher' Cumberland for the severity with which the order was carried out.
Jim O'Sullivan, Yarm, Cleveland.

☐ THE MOST likely explanation stems from the fact that the coat of arms of Sir John Dalrymple, Master of Stair, was 'or, on a saltire azure, nine lozenges of the first' (i.e. a nine of diamonds). After the leader of the MacDonald clan inadvertently failed to sign an oath of loyalty to William III, Dalrymple moved to use this as an excuse to eliminate the leading clan members, in what became known as the Glen Coe massacre. It was Sir John who slipped the death warrants into William's notoriously huge in-tray and tricked the king into signing them. The scandal was not only that the slaughter occurred, but also that, although Dalrymple was charged with treason, he was not tried and was merely dismissed from office three years later. In Scotland today, the holiday caravan is nicknamed the nine of diamonds.
D. R. F. Forsyth, Tunbridge Wells, Kent.

☐ I HAVE a pack of 'Historical Scottish Playing Cards' which offers three possible reasons for this name. Firstly, in the game called Pope Joan, the nine of diamonds is known as the Pope – anti-Christ of the Scottish reformers. Another explanation comes from the game Comette (introduced by Mary Queen of Scots) in which it was the winning card. Due to the fact that so many were ruined by the game, it was called 'the curse of Scotland'. One other possibility is that the nine of diamonds is arranged to form a St Andrew's cross (but then so are the other nines) – 'curse' being a corruption of the word 'cross'.
Joy Bennett, Hull, N. Humberside.

QUESTION: I have read that it was once a capital offence in England to impersonate an Egyptian. Is this true and what were the reasons?

☐ THE WANDERING people, called by themselves Romany, first appeared in England in the early 16th century and were then thought to have come from Egypt. Hence the description 'Egyptians' (and its corruption into 'gypsy') and the legislation against them. Thus in 1530 Henry VIII expelled the 'outlandish people calling themselves Egyptians . . . who used great, subtil and crafty means to deceive the people . . . that they by palmestry could tell men's and women's fortunes'. Later legislation provided that if any 'Egyptians shall remain in this realm or Wales one month . . . it is felony', and it was also felony to disguise oneself as an Egyptian or to be seen in company with them. All the felonies were without benefit of clergy and therefore attracted the death penalty. By the Restoration the offence was still being prosecuted to execution, for Chief Justice Sir Mathew Hale recalled that 'at the Assizes at Bury about 13 were condemned and executed for this offence', and at York Assizes in 1655 four persons were accused of keeping company with vagabonds 'commonly called egiptians', though they were fortunate enough to be acquitted. The statutes were repealed in the 18th century when it was provided that 'all persons pretending to be gypsies, or wandering in the habit or form of Egyptians shall be deemed rogues and vagabonds'.
Sarah Mercer, York.

☐ IN AYLESBURY, seven men and a woman were sentenced to be hanged in 1577 after being found guilty of 'keeping company with Egyptians'.

Roy Price, Maidstone, Kent.

☐ FROM THE Tudor period, parishes were responsible for their own poor relief. Any unemployed travellers were quickly escorted out of the area and into someone else's parish. In 1699 these 'sturdy beggars' were more precisely defined and listed. Among them; any pretending to be scholars making their way to or from university; seafaring men pretending to be returning home after shipwreck; strolling minstrels, actors, fencers and bear-wards; those claiming to be collecting for charities, leperhouses, hospitals or prisons; palmists, conjurors and those impersonating Egyptians (i.e. gypsy fortune-tellers).
(Mr) L. Thorp, Doncaster.

QUESTION: What is the 'Burton' that things go for?

☐ IN 1940, trainee wireless operators in the RAF learned their Morse at the Empress Ballroom, Blackpool. If a trainee failed to pass the test (i.e. failed to read the requisite number of words in the time allowed) he had to attend extra training sessions in the evening. These extra sessions were held in the large room over Montague Burton's shop on the promenade. Thus 'Going to Burton's' or 'Going for a Burton' became the phrase for any sort of failure or disaster.
Ernest F. Evans, Bradford-on-Avon, Wilts.

☐ THE PHRASE stems back to the RAF during the Second World War. The beer drunk by pilots around the Cambridgeshire/Lincolnshire area was brewed by Burtons Ales. Should a pilot not return from a mission, he was said to have 'gone for a Burton', in other words, gone down to the pub. This got over the problem of having to admit the loss of a fellow pilot, and perhaps tempt fate.
Peter May, London SE9.

☐ THIS originates from an advertising campaign for Burton Ale. The advert showed a football team photograph –

however, amidst their ranks was a gap where one team member was obviously missing. The slogan below read: 'He's gone for a Burton'.
Cliff Lovelock, Shepperton, Middx.

QUESTION: Why are Arndale centres so named?

☐ 'ARNDALE' is derived from the first name of one of the founders of the firm, and the surname of the other: ARNold Hagenbach, and Sam ChippenDALE.
Simon Green, Park Grove, Hull.

☐ THE Arndale company, founded in Bradford in 1950, was one of the first to specialise in shopping developments and the only one of any size not run from London. It began by developing small parades of shops in Yorkshire and neighbouring counties. Its first big operation was the redevelopment of Jarrow town centre in 1958. The story of this enterprise and the early work of the company is told in *The Property Boom*, by Oliver Marriot (1967). Chippendale fronted the operation, buying derelict pieces of backland close to existing shopping centres and negotiating with councils for partnership in comprehensive redevelopment. One of his major assets was his ability to exploit his Yorkshire background (born in Osset, a descendant of the well-known furniture maker) and his manner with local councillors. To quote Marriot: 'North country councillors were suspicious in their encounters with developers and estate agents from London. The Borough Treasurer of Jarrow spoke admiringly of Chippendale. "He was a bit blunt and outspoken and he impressed some of my councillors who were more than a little difficult to impress. You see he spoke a language we understood".' And of course he made sure that his deals were financially favourable to Arndale – absurdly so in the case of Jarrow. Hagenbach, the minor partner, was a third generation Swiss baker from Wakefield. After the

war he sold his chain of baker's shops, although they continued to trade under the Hagenbach name for many years. Chippendale died only recently.
Peter Edwards, Senior Lecturer in Urban Planning, Oxford Polytechnic.

☐ ARNDALE is an acronym for Architecturally Revolting Nonsensical Depressive Artless Ludicrous Eyesore.
Laura Scale, Prestwich, Manchester.

QUESTION: Can anybody complete the long-forgotten Cockney alphabet (A for 'orses, G for police, etc) that I learned as a boy?

☐ THE COCKNEY alphabet is essentially a set of oral puns which lose most of their wit in print. Far from being long-forgotten, it is still evolving in the oral tradition.
P. Stephenson, Buxton, Derbyshire.

☐ ERIC Partridge's 1961 book, *Comic Alphabets*, documents many versions, which he dates back to bored signallers in the 1914–18 war playing about with their 'signalese' phonetic alphabet.
Graham Gooday, Aberdeen.

☐ A for 'orses; cadopear; ism; Gardner. B for lamb; brooke; strength; honey. C for 'th' Highlanders; looking; yourself; ships. D for dumb; ential; rent; salmon; mation; Just Men. E for brick; Adam; so careful; Bartok; lin Waugh. F for vescent; yours; calf; so nice. G for Indian; police; goodness sake. H for himself; retirement; teen. I for Novello; the engine; luting. J for oranges. K for tea; restaurant; teria; nuts; ances. L for leather; goblin; fairy. M for sis; size; ever blowing bubbles. N for lope; mation; a stretch, duration etc; a penny; cement; Pasha. O for the wings of a dove; the rainbow; coat; my dead body; sexed; joyed. P for ration. Q

for a bus; a song; billiards; everything. **R** for mo; bitter; Askey; English; ritis. **S** for you. **T** for two; aching; golf. **U** for me; instance; Fox; ia; nerve. **V** for France; voce; hospital; De Gaulle; the difference. **W** for a quid; quits. **X** for breakfast. **Y** for mistress; sake me; get me; husband. **Z** for breezes; 'e to do it, maister.
Peter Stewart, Epsom, Surrey.

QUESTION: What is the origin of the 'Waiter, there's a fly in my soup' joke?

□ A NUMBER of 'Waiter . . .' jokes are attributed to the notoriously rude waiters at Lindy's Restaurant in New York, whose replies include: 'It's possible. The chef used to be a tailor' and 'Don't worry. How much soup can a fly drink?' Lindy's was started in August 1921 by Leo Lindemann and was as famous for the backchat of its waiters as for its clientele of comics, gangsters, show-biz stars and other celebrities. Among examples of repartee recorded on their menu (always entailing criticism of the customer and/or the food) are some which have gone on to become almost traditional: 'Waiter, do you serve shrimps here?' Lindy's waiter: 'Sure. We don't care how tall you are. Sit down.' and 'Waiter, this coffee tastes like tea.' Lindy's waiter: 'Forgive me, sir. I must have given you the hot chocolate by mistake.'
Stuart Mealing, Talaton, Exeter.

□ IN HER anthology, *One Hundred Renaissance Jokes*, Barbara Bowen identifies a Latin epigram by Sir Thomas More as a likely forerunner. At a banquet, a guest removes some flies from the loving-cup, drinks, then replaces them, before passing it on with the remark: 'I don't like flies myself, but perhaps some of you chaps do.'
Mike Heath, Alton, Hants.

QUESTION: What is the origin of the word 'bus'?

□ THE EARLIEST known use of public transport within towns occurred in Nantes in western France in 1827. It was the idea of the enterprising Monsieur Omnès, who coined the name Omnibus as a pun, to indicate both the purpose and the name of the instigator of this service. Since, in Latin, *omnibus* is the plural form of both the dative and ablative cases of the word *omnes* (all), *omnibus* originally meant either 'for everybody' (dative) or by 'Omnès' (ablative). Later, the word was taken into English, and eventually abbreviated to 'bus' in both languages, though in French it first passed through the modification 'autobus' with the invention of the internal combustion engine. Incidentally, the word 'omnibus' is still used in modern French in a transport context, but it now designates a train which stops at all stations.

John Mitchell, Southampton.

QUESTION: The Book of Revelation (ch 13 v 18) says that the mark of the beast is six hundred and sixty-six. What sort of mark would that be? In Roman numerals the number is DCLXVI.

□ 'LET HIM who has wisdom count the number of the beast, for the number of the beast is the number of a man.' In Greek (in which the Book of Revelation was written) and also in Hebrew, there were originally no numerals – so individual letters were used to symbolise them. Alpha and aleph stood for one, beta and beth for two, etc. When 10 was reached (iota and iod) the numbers then proceeded in decades, kappa and caph for 20, etc. and similarly when the tens were exhausted letters stood in for 100, 200, etc. One of the intriguing effects of this system is that every word has a numerical equivalent which can be obtained by adding together the values of its letters. Since the number of the

beast is the number of a man, it is logical that the number 666 stands for some individual. The most plausible candidate seems to be the Roman Emperor, Nero, since when his name is written as Neron Caesar in Hebrew the characters make up the magic total. (There are other clues in the text to support this identification and Nero's persecution of Christians after the fire of Rome would also be likely to make him and the Anti-Christ one and the same person in early Christian eyes.) There is no biblical foundation to suggest that the mark of the beast (placed on his follower's foreheads) is actually the number 666. This is simply an idea that was popularised by the horror film, *The Omen*. Since it is written 'that no man could buy and sell except that he had the mark of the beast upon him' many fundamentalist Christians in the United States look with suspicion on the security holograms of their credit cards. (And who's to say they're so very far from wrong, eh?)
W. A. Saunders, London.

☐ THE PICTURE described is of two beasts – the first (ch 13 vv 1-10) out of the sea (i.e. foreign, the Roman imperial power); the second (ch 13 vv 11-18) out of the land (i.e. the indigenous, the local ruling Asian council). The graphic imagery is the language of Jewish apocalyptic, in this case deliberately borrowing from the beasts of Daniel ch 7 v 3f. The Emperor Domitian had recently declared that he was to be known as Dominus et Deus ('ruler and God') – hence the beast having a blasphemous name (Rev. ch 13 v 3). The strange comment about the fatal wound to one head of the beast (ch 13 v 3) refers to the suicide of Nero. The second beast (i.e. the Asian Council) derived its authority from Rome . . . There is also a possible reference to the inscriptions on Domitian's coins, which were in Latin 'Imperator Caesar Domitianus Augustus Germanicus', or in Greek 'Autokrator Kaisar Dometianos Sebastos Germanikos', which, if abbreviated to 'A KAI DOMET SEB GE' would add up to 666. So the reference to the mark of the beast is probably a reference to the persecution of Christians by Domitian at the end of the 1st century AD: either they denied Christ and gave their loyalty to the Emperor (false 'dominus et deus') or they faced death. There have been numerous attempts over the centuries to find a current 'Antichrist'. Some have even tried to make it fit Henry Kissinger or the EEC. Any ideas on new candidates?

(Rev.) Anthony E. Buglass, Amble, Northumberland.

☐ THE CONTRIBUTIONS so far on this topic remind me of an explanation that was current during the last war. This sought to prove that Adolf Hitler was indeed the Beast. The proof required the number 100 to be given to the first letter of the alphabet, 101 to B, 102 to C, and so on, finishing with 125 for Z. By simply totalling the numbers appropriate to the letters of Adolf's surname, lo and behold, we finish with 666. Ingenious, if nothing else.

George Harrison, Stretford, Manchester.

☐ I AM MUCH amused by the deep theorising over this. The answer is simple. The Jews believed the number seven to be the number of perfection, since God created the world in seven days. This is why the dates of Jewish festivals reflect a pattern of seven. The idea was carried over into early Christian belief and is much used in Revelation, e.g. seven churches, seven bowls, seven seals. To say, then, that the mark of the beast is 666 declares that it has failed to reach perfection and, although powerful, is not God.

(Miss) H Fitch, Theydon Bois, Essex.

QUESTION: Why is there a © mark on the new £5 note? I had planned to run off a few million but am worried that I may contravene the copyright laws.

☐ THE © symbol protects the illustrations, and prevents copyists from escaping serious penalties by claiming their handiwork as 'art'. If the questioner wants to avoid breach of copyright and merely commit forgery, he should first commission his own artwork. Incidentally, one wonders if Mr Frankie Howerd gave permission for his likeness to be reproduced on the back of the new £5 note.

Tessa Kamara, Ealing, London W13.

☐ THE Forgery and Counterfeiting Act of 1981 makes it an offence to reproduce Bank of England notes without permission, so one could argue that the copyright symbol is unnecessary. However, the Bank does own the copyright on all its notes and the copyright symbol is intended to act as an explicit warning signal against inadvertent unauthorised reproduction.

S. J. R. Sullivan, Assistant to the Chief of the Banking Department, Bank of England, London EC2.

QUESTION: Why, after drinking a certain quantity of wine, does one find that the room is spinning? And why always clockwise?

☐ THE spinning sensation must be caused by alcohol upsetting the semi-circular canals of the inner ear, which sense balance. This effect can also occur when these organs become infected, resulting in a spinning sensation, loss of balance, nausea and vomiting. One of us noticed, when taking a bath in a Buenos Aires hotel while drinking several cans of lager that: (a) the water drained in an anti-clockwise direction; (b) the bathroom appeared to spin anti-clockwise. Of course, both have a clockwise sense in the northern hemisphere. This is a well-documented feature observed in wind and oceanic currents; the 'coriolis force' caused by the earth's rotation. We are keen to continue our studies of this phenomenon and would be grateful for funding towards an equatorial expedition (and several bottles of whisky) to shed more light on this interesting puzzle.

(Drs) Chris Ward and Allister Rees, London W7.

☐ THE particular type of alcohol in wine erodes the rivets holding your balancing gyroscope in place. Fortunately for our long-term sense of balance, the rivets are not permanently destroyed. A man with a hammer always arrives to repair them first thing next morning.
Steven Thomson, London W6.

QUESTION: Why do bagels have a hole in them? Why are they boiled before baking?

☐ ALTHOUGH the people living in the small Jewish villages in Russia had grown used to the constant persecutions of the Tsars, there was one time when a particularly cruel Tsar arose. Not only did he demand a tenth of all the bread they baked, but he demanded that the royal portion should come from the middle of each loaf, so ruining it. The wise men of Chelm got together to discuss how to overcome this terrible burden. Eventually, they came upon a brilliant idea. They baked small, round loaves of bread, with a hole in the middle. The hole was exactly one tenth the size of the rest of the loaf. When the Tsar's soldiers came to collect the royal tithe, the wise men of Chelm presented them with the holes, pointing out that this was the middle portion of the loaf, just as the Tsar had instructed. The soldiers couldn't argue with this and went away empty-handed. Incidentally, in Israel, bagels have much larger holes, as a protest against the high taxation in that country,
Brian Rose, Pinner, Middlesex.

☐ THE explanations of why a bagel is dipped in boiling water and why it has a hole in the middle are interconnected. First, the boiling water has a little sugar added to it, which serves to glaze the dough, and give it a satisfying surface texture when baked. The heat of the water expands the bubbles in the dough, making it light and airy. The effect is limited to areas near the surface, which is the reason for the bagel's toroidal shape. It is to maximise the surface area in relation to volume. A roll or 'bap' treated in this fashion would have a leaden centre.

Fred Cairns, Woburn Green, Bucks.

☐ FRED CAIRNS is mistaken in his explanation of why bagels are boiled before baking. According to Harold McGee's *On Food and Cooking*, moistening dough causes surface starch to gelatinise; when baked, the gelatinised starch turns into a brown, glossy crust. Some breads are sprayed with water (or brushed with beaten egg) to produce the same effect. Presumably, bagels are boiled so that more of the starch will gelatinise, thus producing a thicker crust. The tiny amount of sugar or malt added to the water may aid formation of the crust, but it is not solely or even principally responsible for it.

Richard Ehrlich, London NW5.

☐ BAGELS (and when my Campaign For Real Yiddish gets going the spelling will revert to the non-American 'beigel') are not, as they are usually described, Jewish doughnuts but rather misshapen Jewish croissants. And not so Jewish at that. They were originally cooked in Vienna to celebrate the relief of the Turkish siege of that city in 1529. The symbol of the Muslim Turks was a crescent, and the beigel was cooked in that shape. Indeed, in any well-crafted beigel you can see where the two crescent ends have been joined together.

John Diamond, London EC1.

☐ JOHN DIAMOND'S explanation is half-baked. Bagels were indeed baked to celebrate the relief of Vienna from the Turks – but in 1683, not 1529. The commander of the liberating troops who saved Christian Europe from the Infidel was Jan Sobieski, the Polish king and military genius. Locals were so grateful that they rushed forward to kiss his stirrup ('Bügel'

in German) as he passed on horseback. Jewish bakers
prepared a special stirrup-shaped bread to mark the occasion; the name has degenerated from 'Bügel' to 'Bagel'.
Peter Varey, Ullesthorpe, Leics.

**QUESTION: Where, when and by whom were semi-
detached houses first built?**

☐ I DO NOT know where the first semi-detached house was
built but I have it on reliable authority that the second one
was built just next door to the first.
George James, Shepperton, Middx.

☐ THE ORIGIN of the semi-detached house, at least in London, is explained in *The Book of London*, which I edited for
Weidenfeld last year. The Georgian terrace held sway until
the last decade of the 18th century, when inflationary
pressures pushed up building costs and left some terraces
uncompleted – similar to the problems today in Docklands.
Building houses in self-contained pairs meant that it was
easier to stop when the money ran out. The architect and
developer, Michael Searles, is credited with London's ear-

liest semis, built in Kennington Park Road in the early 1790s. He followed these with a development in Greenwich and the Paragon in Blackheath. Then, as now, south London was at the cutting edge of innovation.
Michael Leapman, London SW8.

☐ MICHAEL Leapman is nearly there – but not quite. Architect Michael Searles (a Greenwich man) may well have been inspired by the pair of houses built in Blackheath in 1776 by Thoman Gayfere and John Groves, both of Westminster. The houses, which stand today on the west edge of the Heath and are known as Lydia and Sherwell are, by legend, the first semi-detached houses certainly in London. That is, if you take the meaning of semi-detached to be two houses consciously-designed to look from a distance like one. Pevsner/Cherry in their book, *London 2: South*, give the Gayfere/Groves houses the accolade. It is a credit which we at the Blackheath Society will stoutly defend. Searles's first semis followed about 30 years later. But if it is the terrace form in question then Searles is your man.
Neil Rhind for The Blackheath Society, London SE5.

☐ SORRY, Blackheath! Richard Gillow of Lancaster (1734–1811) was designing 'semis' or pairs of houses in that town as early as 1758/9, in Moor Lane. The earliest identifiable surviving pair is that built in 1760 at Fleet Bridge (now facing the bus station and partly demolished) for Captain Henry Fell. These are very similar to a pair in St Leonardsgate which may be the buildings designed by Gillow in 1765/6 for Edward Salisbury. Captain Fell occupied one of his houses himself but the others were built to be let. Gillow obtained estimates of £110 for building William Braithwaite's houses in Moor Lane in 1759 and reckoned they would let for £4 per annum each. *Pace* Pevsner, no legend here: the evidence is in the Gillow archives in Westminster Public Library. Richard Gillow was the son of the founder of the cabinet-making dynasty, and seems to have

studied architecture in London. From 1757 to the 1770s he provided designs for numerous public and private buildings in the Lancaster area. The architectural work of Richard Gillow was the subject of my dissertation at Cambridge in 1982. I used the Gillow archives to establish beyond doubt that Richard Gillow designed a considerable number of buildings in this period.
P. A. Harrison, London SW16.

☐ SORRY, Blackheath! Sorry, Richard Gillow of Lancaster. What must surely be counted as the first pair of semi-detached houses, nos 808–810 Tottenham High Road, London N17, date from 1715–1725 – thus predating Gillow's work by something like 50 years. This pair of houses makes a noble and remarkably balanced visual ensemble still, despite later shopfronts. For an illustration see Dan Cruickshank and Peter Wyld's fascinating *London: the Art of Georgian Building.*
Philip Maher, Marston, Oxford.

☐ IT WAS always my belief that the semi-detached dwelling originated in the ancient Inca civilisation of South America. This novel idea greatly impressed the Spanish Conquistadores, who brought the concept to Europe in the 16th century, and gave it the name 'Casa Doble'.
Vaughan R. Hully, Warley, W Midlands.

☐ SUMMERSON'S Georgian London states that the Eyre Estate in St John's Wood 'was the first part of London, and indeed of any other town, to abandon the terrace house for the semi-detached villa – a revolution of striking significance and far-reaching effect.' One reason why the semi-detached house was so frequently built between the wars was that motor buses could still operate profitably in new, less densely developed suburbs where passenger loadings would have been too low to justify building new tramways and railways. Another reason was that Town and Country

Planning zoning introduced in new suburbs from 1909 onwards provided for different residential areas to be developed at varying densities, usually between 4 and 12 houses per acre. Plots in the middle zones were too small for detached houses but too large for terraces and therefore most suitable for semi-detached houses. The archetypal outer London semi may appear more prevalent than it really is because some developers erected semi-detached houses on the principal main road frontages but built terraces in the hinterland.
John Tarling, London SW15.

☐ THE semi-detached houses identified by your correspondents are all far too modern. Here in Cornwall we have a pair of semis dating from the Roman occupation of Britain, in the 2nd and 3rd centuries AD. The stone-walled village of Chysauster near Penzance had the remains of a house which clearly takes the form of two semi-detached dwellings.
D. Stewart, Helston, Cornwall.

☐ I THINK Warwick can go one better than Blackheath, Lancaster and Tottenham in that it can boast a pair of semi-detached houses which date from the late 1690s. The impressive building, which stands near the site of the old Northgate into the town, looks like one house, but is in fact two, divided by a central carriageway.
Amanda Clarke, Warwick.

☐ IF a semi-detached house is one which was designed as a symmetrically arranged pair there are several surviving examples in Coventry, dating back at least to the 14th century. Nos 169–170 Spon Street, Coventry, which was repaired under the supervision of the architect F. W. B. Charles in 1969–70 for the City of Coventry under the Spon Street Townscape scheme, is a good example of 14th-century date. Further along Spon Street is a 16th-century three-storey pair of town houses from 8–10 Much Park

Street which was dismantled and reconstructed by Mr Charles on its present site in 1971–74. Both these examples had houses built up against them, as the street frontage filled up and we feel sure that there must be many earlier examples which have become absorbed within later terraced development along urban streets. On the principle of originally detached, subsequently attached, we would be interested in hearing how common this type of 'semi' was in medieval towns.

George Demidowicz, Conservation Officer, City of Coventry.

QUESTION: In the gents where I work, there is both a hot-air hand drier and a supply of paper towels. On ecological grounds which should I use? Useful data: The paper is approx 400mm × 250mm and is not apparently recycled, being white and soft. The hot-air drier functions in 40-second bursts, and has specifications 2.11-2.51 kw and 50 Hz.

☐ THE PAPER towel uses approximately 0.0003 per cent of a standard Norwegian fir tree while the hot-air drier uses some 0.019kw hours of electricity, but as the use of the hot-air drier ends up with you drying your hands on your trousers anyway, why not really help the environment by cutting out the first two alternative stages completely?

Richard L Hutchinson, Churchill, Avon.

☐ SO WE can deal with figures that one can get a feel for, I have considered 1,000 people drying their hands, either using 1,000 pieces of paper or 1,000 40-second bursts of the air drier. Let us first consider the towels. A thousand paper towels weigh about 3kg. When all the fuels and electricity used for production, transportation, heating and lighting during the 'processing of paper' are aggregated, the energy cost of paper towels is about 25J/kg. So in 'energy' terms the towels cost about 75MJ (21kwh, a 1kw machine run continuously for 21 hours). Now for the hot-air drier. One thousand bursts of 40 seconds each is about 11 hours at a continuous load of 2.31KW (average of 2.11 and 2.51). This is about 25 KWh, however, assuming this is produced by a coal-fired power station (with a maximum efficiency of about 36 per cent) the total energy input required would be about 70KWh 252MJ. This does not tackle the fact that the hot-air drier causes about three times as much CO_2 to be given off, the disposal of the towels (although they could be recycled) or indeed the 'energy' cost of producing the air blower itself. However, it does seem that using the paper towels is more ecologically sound in terms of 'energy' (and not money, for a change).

Richard Baker, Energy Engineer, Redbridge, Essex.

☐ FOR A brilliant and extremely funny discussion of the paper towel over the hot-air drier – on ecological grounds, too – see chapter 11 of Nicholson Baker's book, *The Mezzanine* (Granta, 1989).

Peter Kaan, Topsham, Devon.

QUESTION: Where did Somerset Maugham get the title, *The Moon and Sixpence,* for his novel?

☐ ROBERT Lorin Calder, in *W. Somerset Maugham and the Quest for Freedom* (1972), gives the following explanation. The *Times Literary Supplement*, in reviewing *Of Human Bondage*, had written: 'Like so many young men he [Philip] was so busy yearning for the moon that he never saw the sixpence at his feet.' Somerset Maugham adopted the phrase as the title of his next novel. The author explained its meaning in a note which was intended to precede the text, but which did not appear, 'In his childhood he was urged to make merry over the man who, looking for the moon, missed the sixpence at his feet, but having reached years of maturity

he is not so sure that this was so great an absurdity as he was bidden to believe. Let him who will pick up the sixpence; to pursue the moon seems the most amusing diversion.'
Ronald H. Bond, Chelmsford, Essex.

QUESTION: If I were to travel a complete circuit of the M25 how many miles would I save by driving anti-clockwise as opposed to clockwise?

☐ THE DISTANCE saved is not dependent on the length of the circuit but only on the width of the separation between the two carriageways. In fact it is 2π times the average separation. The answer depends on which lane the driver uses. In the inside lane, supposing each lane is 3 metres wide and the central reservation is 6 metres across the distance saving is $2\pi \times ((5 \times 3) + 6) = 142$ metres. Observation shows, though, that in practice no one uses the inside lane on the M25. More probably, the journeys will be made in the two 'fast' lanes, which are separated by just 9 metres. This means a saving of $2\pi \times 9$, or only 57 metres out of a circuit length of roughly 200 kilometres.
Peter Telford, Redhill, Surrey.

☐ PETER TELFORD is much mistaken. His formula would only apply if the route round the M25 formed a perfect circle, which it does not. Part of this motorway may be in circular form but there will be straight sections. Assuming that these were to turn off at right angles the distance saved would be eight times the separation, as opposed to 6.28 times the separation for the circle. So the factors will change constantly, depending on the radius of the road at any given point. Theoretically it is almost impossible to calculate the exact mileage saved, and the only practical way is to drive round both routes and take the difference in distances. However, I can assure you that the distance saved would be a very small fraction of the actual distance travelled.
Christiaan Jonkers, Stourbridge, W. Midlands.

☐ I MUST defend Peter Telford and challenge Christiaan Jonkers. The distance saved is indeed twice π times the average separation, and can be proved mathematically to be so. Further, the circuit does not have to be a circle, or anything like one. All that is needed is that the curve followed by the motorway be sufficiently smooth (that is, that the curves have large radius compared to the turning circle of the car), and motorways with sharp corners are not too popular with the Department of Transport. Whether or not there are straight sections is a complete red herring. Actually, there is just one thing that might disturb the calculations. They do assume that the motorway is flat (planar). But I doubt that the ups and downs affect the final answer all that much, since again they are never too drastic.
(Dr) Peter McMullen, Dept of Mathematics, University College, London.

☐ MUCH as I dislike disagreeing with a colleague, I feel that I must do so. Dr McMullen ignores an important factor. A simple consequence of Pythagoras's theorem is that overtaking manoeuvres usually result in drivers travelling further. Due to this, there can be considerable variability in the total distance travelled between successive circuits of a ring road, even for journeys made in the same direction. Although pure mathematics could be used to estimate the effects this would have on journeys around the M25, perhaps someone should experiment.
(Dr) Stephen Gallivan, Dept of Statistical Research, University College, London WC1.

☐ IF WE allow the earth to be a perfect sphere then the quantity twice π times the carriageway separation is too much. A correction equal to four times π times the area of London (i.e. enclosed by the M25) divided by the area of the earth must be subtracted.
Jonathan Fine, Huntingdon, Cambs.

☐ YOU cannot travel a complete circuit of the M25. The motorway gives way to the A282 at the approaches to the Dartford Tunnel.
T. J. Allen, Hindhead, Surrey.

☐ A FRIEND and I decided to experiment. We first calibrated our milometers to make certain they read the same distance for a stretch of road, and then I drove clockwise and my friend anti-clockwise on the M25. Our starting and finishing point was the South Mimms service station. The result was surprising: clockwise 120.30 miles, anti-clockwise 120.80 miles. We agreed that we would stay in the slow lane as far as possible, only moving to the middle lane when appropriate. Neither of us used the outer, fast lane. However, the discrepancy of 0.5 miles seems to have occurred because of a diversion on the anti-clockwise circuit, immediately south of the Dartford Tunnel. So, at the moment, it is a shorter journey to take the clockwise carriageway, especially if travelling to Kent or Essex.
Penelope Edwards, E. Finchley, London N2.

☐ I FEAR that Penelope Edwards and her friend have wasted both time and money in driving round the M25. A car's odometer only measures to the nearest 0.1 mile and, even if you can estimate distances by the partial change of the numbers, it cannot be better than 0.05 miles. Calibrating the odometers of the two cars against one another will not help because of this basic inaccuracy in the odometer's mechanism. If the distance over which they drove to calibrate them was 10 miles, then their calibration will be accurate to 0.05 miles in 10 miles, equivalent to 0.6 miles over the complete 120-mile trip; greater than the difference they found. Even if they had used the same car for the two trips, removing the need for calibration, it is unlikely that the result would be any more reliable, since the same trip

made in the same car will not necessarily give the same measured distance every time. The basic problem is one that affects every scientist or engineer carrying out a measurement; the equipment must be able to measure smaller than the quantity being measured. Otherwise, it's like using a tape measure to find the diameter of a human hair.
Dudley Turner, Westerham, Kent.

QUESTION: Who was 'nosey' Parker?

☐ THE FIRST supplement to the *Oxford English Dictionary* credits Compton Mackenzie with the earliest use of the expression in his 1912 novel, *Carnival*: 'I saw you go off with a fellah.' 'What of it, Mr Nosey Parker?' This was only two years after the earliest cited example of 'nosey' in the sense of 'inquisitive, curious', as used by H. G. Wells in *The History of Mr Polly*. So the expression seems to have derived from early 20th-century slang. However, I well remember as a lad an illustrated and informative item a magazine which said that the original Nosey Parker was Matthew Parker, Elizabeth I's first Archbishop of Canterbury. I can find no confirmation of this in the hagiographic entry on him in the *Dictionary Of National Biography* or any other reference work I have been able to consult. The *OED* would have us believe that 'nosey' could not have been used in any sense as early as the 16th century: 1, 'One who has a large nose' is apparently not known before 1788; 2, 'Evil smelling', 1836; 3, 'Fragrant', 1892; 4, 'Sensitive to bad smells', 1894.
(Dr) Richard Dutton, Dept of English, Lancaster University.

QUESTION: Could anyone tell me what Wittgenstein was doing in Newcastle in the 1940s and where he was living?

☐ ACCORDING to Anthony Kenny in his book, *Wittgenstein,*

the philosopher was working as a medical orderly in the clinical research laboratory at the Royal Victoria Infirmary in Newcastle upon Tyne during the Second World War. According to Norman Malcolm's footnote to one of Wittgenstein's letters from Newcastle, printed in Malcolm's *Ludwig Wittgenstein: A Memoir* (pp. 91–2), Wittgenstein was invited to work with a Dr R. T. Grant in the laboratory, where he studied the relationship between breathing and pulse, using himself as a guinea pig.

Robert Edwards, Hornchurch, Essex.

QUESTION: Why does eating asparagus make your urine smell?

☐ ASPARAGUS possesses a group of naturally-occurring sulphur-containing compounds, the most important of which has been named asparagusic acid. When these compounds are broken down in the body, a number of chemicals (dimethyl disulphide, dimethyldisulphide, bis(methylthio)-methane, dimethylsulphoxide, dimethylsulphone) are formed. Together these produce the typical 'rotten' or 'boiling cabbage' odour to which the questioner refers. Not all individuals produce such compounds. Studies by Dr Steven Mitchell and colleagues, for example, show that just under half of the UK population exhibit this characteristic trait, which remains with a subject for virtually a lifetime, irrespective of changes in social and environmental conditions. While other foods, notably onion and cabbage, also contain sulphurous compounds, these have different structures to those in asparagus, are not broken down in the body in the same way and do not cause the problem referred to.

Dr G. R. Fenwick, AFRC, Institute of Food Research, Norwich.

QUESTION: Why are there 18 holes on a golf course?

☐ BY THE mid-18th century, the golfers of St Andrews had achieved the reputation of being the pacesetters and unofficial authorities on the game, largely as a result of an open competition organised by the Society of St Andrews for which a trophy, in the form of a silver club, was presented. The success of the contest established St Andrews as the premier golfing town and when, in 1764, the society changed its course from 12 holes to 18, other clubs followed suit. Hence, 18 holes soon became the standard for a full course. Before then, the number of holes varied from club to club, due partly to the amount of land available. The golfers of St Andrews, restricted by the narrow strip of duneland on which the course was built, utilised their 12 holes by playing 11 holes 'going out' and then retracing their steps and playing 11 holes 'home', over the same fairways in a reverse direction, using 10 of the holes twice. Their 'round' was thus 22 holes but when the society decided to turn the first four holes into two, the round was reduced to 18 holes.
John Beetham, Cheadle, Cheshire.

QUESTION: How is caffeine removed from coffee?

☐ THE BEST method for decaffeinating coffee beans is to use carbon dioxide, which is usually a gas, but under high pressure takes on another form known as a 'supercritical fluid'. Such fluids combine the features of liquids and gases in an intriguing manner. Supercritical carbon dioxide has the ability to dissolve solids. The fluid is passed over the coffee beans, the caffeine dissolves and can then be recovered by lowering the pressure and turning the supercritical fluid back into a gas. The caffeine-free beans are then roasted. Supercritical carbon dioxide has the advantage that it is non-toxic and leaves no residue behind. The decaffeination process is carried out in a sealed system and the gas

recycled. There is minimal loss of carbon dioxide into the atmosphere where it could add to the greenhouse effect.
Margaret Jobling and Mark Simmons, Chemistry Department, University of Nottingham.

☐ MARGARET Jobling and Mark Simmons have given only a partial answer. Any solvent which would dissolve out the caffeine from the coffee without dissolving out anything else could be used. Carbon dioxide, as a supercritical fluid, is one liquid which can be used. Another is methylene chloride, and I believe that it is this which is more frequently used. Carbon dioxide is of low toxicity and, being volatile, disappears completely from the coffee afterwards. But carbon dioxide under high pressure is difficult and therefore expensive to handle. Methylene chloride, on the other hand, is easy to handle, being a liquid at normal temperatures. It is also of low volatility (by comparison with carbon dioxide) and therefore does not disappear completely from the coffee after doing its job. It is also rather toxic. If I were going to drink decaffeinated coffee, I would want to know what had been used to remove the caffeine, and whether there was any of it left in the coffee. This information seems to be absent from the labels.
Mark Harrison, Harringay, London.

☐ AN AMERICAN friend told my mother that one should only buy decaffeinated coffee when the label says 'Naturally Decaffeinated' and not when the label reads merely 'Decaffeinated', as the latter has involved a more toxic decaffeinating process. As is often the case, the good old public remains firmly in the dark on these matters while the manufacturers cover themselves, but in secret.
Karin Padgham, London W6.

QUESTION: Is there any evidence to support the theory that the bandleader, Glenn Miller, did not die in a plane

crash but was in fact murdered in the Pigalle district of Paris and that the truth was hidden by the authorities for reasons of wartime morale?

☐ AT THE time of Glenn Miller's disappearance I was a radar operator on the east coast. I can remember going on watch when Filter Room was querying plots on a VIP ident track which appeared to be deviating from its expected course. The following day we heard the VIP had been Glenn Miller. I believe he was alone. There was a rumour that he was trying to get back to America and didn't make it.
(Mrs) Dorothy Carter, Buchie, Banffshire.

☐ THE FLIGHT that Glenn Miller reputedly took was not a scheduled flight. My father, E. F. Woods, was a communications engineer, serving in Eisenhower's SHAEF staff operating from Brussels. He and his team were scheduled to fly back to the UK when the flight was requisitioned by the Glenn Miller Band. The plane of course vanished. After the war he made several attempts to get his story published and the 'fictional' story corrected. The attempts failed. He, and the others concerned, were certain there was a mystery and I would be very interested to hear of any more clues.
(Dr) Mike Woods, Baildon, Bradford

☐ MILLER was flying *to* the continent, not *from* it. In fact to Paris and not from Brussels to England. There were no scheduled flights in 1944. The aircraft was a single-engined Norseman carrying Miller, an Army Air Corps colonel and the pilot. The weather on Friday, December 15, 1944 was bad with poor visibility. Miller was advised not to make the flight. No radio communication took place, so the reasons for crashing are not explained; mechanical failure or the weather are the most likely.
Neale Johnson, Essendine, nr Stamford, Lincs.

QUESTION: The owl and the pussycat 'dined upon mince/and slices of quince/which they ate with a runcible spoon'. What is a runcible spoon?

☐ MANY of Edward Lear's poems have nonsensical references to his daily life. The 'runcible' spoon was Lear's way of teasing his friend, George Runcy. Runcy had very modern views (for his day) on bringing up children and believed, among other things, that they should be encouraged to feed themselves as early as possible. To this end George Runcy designed a spoon that had the hollow part for food curved towards the handle at 90°, thereby enabling the child to insert the spoon into its mouth end-on, without having to bend its wrist. This made eating with the spoon much easier and Runcy used the spoon to teach all of his children to eat. This type of spoon can still be bought in department stores, but George Runcy, to my knowledge, was never credited with its invention.
Merlin Shepherd, Penarth, S Glamorgan.

☐ AT THE TIME Edward Lear wrote his nonsense verses, he was employed by the Earl of Derby at Knowsley Hall. He fastened upon the adjective 'runcible' for the type of spoon to be used by the Owl and the Pussycat from the character Robert Runcie, who was the Chief Under Butler at the hall in 1832. Runcie was responsible for cleaning the silver spoons. This is alluded to in an obscure footnote to C. J. Jackson's, 'The Spoon and its History', in *Archaeologica* 1892.
C. C. A. Glossop, Worcester.

☐ NEITHER of the suggested derivations of runcible spoon is very convincing, as 'runcible' as a general-purpose nonsense adjective is not confined to spoons in Lear's verse: the Pobble's Aunt Jobisa possessed a runcible cat, with crimson whiskers. Runcible objects (spoons or cats) exist no more than pobbles or feline-hiboutic matrimony.
Michael G. Myer, Cambridge.

QUESTION: Is it possible: a 50,000-word novel that does not use the letter 'e'?

☐ IN 1939 an American author, Ernest Vincent Wright, produced a book called *Gadsby*, consisting of almost 300 pages, in which no word contained the vowel 'e'. To achieve this he taped down the 'e' key on his typewriter, rendering it unusable. Choosing his words meticulously, he managed to complete the tome in less than six months, in a style and syntax that was obviously strained. Copies of the original are now much sought after by bibliofiles.
Mike Hurley, Doncaster, S Yorks.

☐ TH- FIRST s-nt-nc- of *Gadsby* r-ads: 'If Youth, throughout all history, had had a champion to stand up for it; to show a doubting world that a child can think; and. possibly, do it practically; you wouldn't constantly run across folks today who claim that "a child don't know anything".' In a s-nt-nc- of this l-ngth, th- l-tt-r '-' could be -xp-ct-d to app-ar 23 tim-s, bas-d on av-rag- charact-r fr-qu-ncy.
Simon Gray, Sh-ffi-ld.

☐ 'A STORY of over 50,000 words without using the letter E' is the subtitle of *Gadsby*. The novel is mentioned in Georges Perec's *History of the Lipogram*. A lipogram — Greek root *leipo* ('I leave') — is any text written without one of more letters of the alphabet; there are records of lipogrammatic poems, essays, plays and prose going back to the sixth century BC. Obviously the task is as difficult as the letter is frequent; which is why in English and French the most interesting one is to leave out is E. Perec himself wrote a thriller, *La Disparition* about the mysterious disappearance of one Anton Voyl, whose surname would be better anglicised as Vowl. The text is studded with show-pieces, including a version of Rimbaud's sonnet, 'Voyelles'. Bizarrely, a translation of *La Disparition* is planned by a translator and publisher who intend to publish an English version that

employs the letter E. There is a lipogrammatic translation extant, but not in print unfortunately. It is interesting to speculate on the possible future translation of Perec's companion-piece, *Les Revenentes*, which makes use of only one vowel throughout.
Harry Gilonis, Herne Hill, London SE24.

☐ AN ENGLISH translation of *La Disparition* was completed in 1988 by my brother, John Lee. The translation, which also eschews using the letter 'e', was given a full-page feature in the *Times Literary Supplement* and has been the subject of a research degree at Marseilles University. Unfortunately the publisher in this country who owns the rights for Perec's works has refused to allow the translation to appear.
Revd. Fr Gerard M. Lee, Wallsend, Tyne and Wear.

QUESTION: Why is it still not possible with modern technology to run very early movie films at a normal speed?

☐ THE simple answer is that it *is* possible to show them at the correct speed on television but it is easier not to bother. The speed alteration requires a separate pass through the replay equipment and, especially these days, time means money. So, when recognisable pictures are easily and quickly available by just getting them out of the vaults and playing them back, an average production budget will not stretch to cover speed correction. To explain why the speed is wrong: Pathé News and Keystone Cops type films were often shot at a rate of approximately 18 frames a second. Today, British television shows pictures at a speed of 25 frames a second. Any film made at 18fps and played back at 25fps will look too fast. This problem is not only true of old films but also new movies as well. Cinema films today are shot at 24 frames a second, so when we see them on television they run 1/25th of a second too fast. Not much to see but certainly enough to hear. All the film stars you have ever heard on TV sound deeper in real life or in the cinema. The problem is worse in America. There television runs at 30 frames a second so their films would run out faster if the speed was not corrected. When shown in America, British films for TV (shot at 25fps not 24fps so as to avoid the problem) also sound fast. The worst I have heard is Alistair Cooke sounding like Pinky and Perky. All that need be done is to copy the film, at whatever speed, on to a modern video tape recorder. Then play the tape back at the correct original speed through a time base corrector or (if the speed alteration is very big) a standards converter. These devices have a computer-controlled memory which does the sums that will make 18 go into 25 without a hiccup. But the side-effect is that the pictures can look a bit fuzzy or blurred when anything moves. As equipment and computers improve, this 'conversion' smeariness lessens but it is still noticeable. The most famous case of blurred pictures was *Dallas*; things have now improved, however. So it is not too hard to play old films at the right speed. It can be done and sometimes is. I am very glad to see that other people notice the difference as well.

S. R. Anthony, Nottingham.

☐ EARLY 9.5mm and 35mm film stocks were exposed by hand-cranking (i.e. advancing the stock through the shutter gate by manually turning the handle), and the exposure of the film was subject to a constantly-varying speed which even the most experienced operators could not perfect. This was compounded by the effect of hand-cranked projectors, where the skill of many projectionists was even more variable. The only practical way to compensate for the variations in speed, would be to analyse short sequences (often just a few frames at a time) and reprint them, either to new stock or to video tape at their modified speed. Given the meticulous nature of this task, I am not aware of any existing

computer software that facilitates the process, although I am sure it is technically possible. The question that has to be asked, of course, is whether the jumpy, jerky classics would not be rendered bland and characterless by such modification. In the light of the movie establishment's outcry over artificial colourisation of black-and-white films many people would argue that they are better left as they are.
Colin Barrett, Milton Keynes.

QUESTION: What happened to Viraj Mendis after he was deported to Sri Lanka?

☐ HE SPENT almost 14 months in Sri Lanka before being given refuge in Germany. He stayed with his family for the first few months in Sri Lanka but was eventually forced into hiding due to pressure from the so-called peacekeeping forces. The presence of a relay of British supporters and the European publicity about his situation only gave him a limited 'insurance policy'. On more than one occasion the military forced their way into the family home to find him; he received several direct threats to his life, and a number of his friends and acquaintances disappeared, to be found later floating down the river or as victims of tyre burnings. One had obviously been tortured to death. It was during this period that his British fiancée joined him and they married – not exactly an idyllic honeymoon on a paradise island, as pictured in the British press. Eventually, after repeated setbacks, Viraj was allowed into Germany as the spouse of an EC national. His wife had moved to Germany, where she had no family or friends, in order to work so that Viraj could join her after six months' separation. Karen and Viraj lived there initially under the supportive umbrella of a group affiliated to the International Network of Local Initiatives with Asylum-seekers, and now have a flat of their own. He is continuing his work with the Tamils in Germany, publicising the intensive bombing of Tamil areas, the use of napalm

and chemical weapons, the continued offering of aid to Sri Lanka by the EC, and the fact that food and medical provisions often do not reach areas of greatest need.
Fr John Methuen, Rector of Hulme, Manchester 15.

QUESTION: What happened to the *Mary Celeste* after she was found abandoned?

☐ SHE was eventually taken back to New York and sold. The new owner sent her to Montevideo with a cargo of lumber. This appears to have been a pretty disastrous voyage: the ship lost some of her cargo and rigging in a storm on the way out and most of her living cargo of horses and mules (and the skipper!) on the return trip. Thereafter, she changed hands frequently, continuing to ply the American coastline and suffering a series of further mishaps. In 1884, she was acquired by one Gilman C. Parker, who, together with co-conspirators, decided to attempt finally to make some profit from the jinxed vessel. She was loaded with a cargo of junk registered as high-class merchandise and insured for $27,000, deliberately grounded on a coral reef in the Haitian Gulf of Gonave and set on fire, after the cargo and crew had been brought ashore. A claim was duly filed but the suspicious insurance companies sent investigators to question the crew. Parker and three of his partners were subsequently tried in Boston on a charge of barratry but freed because of a hung jury, though they never collected their insurance money. Eight months later, Parker died in disrepute and poverty; one of his associates was sent to a lunatic asylum and another committed suicide. The jinx pursued the *Mary Celeste* to the very end. For more details see John Godwin's book, *This Baffling World* (Bantam, 1973).
Philip J Evison, London SW15.

QUESTION: Is it possible to ride zebras the way we ride horses?

☐ MIRIAM Rothschild, in her book about her uncle, Walter Rothschild, describes how, in November 1894, he introduced zebras to his Tring estate and broke them in with difficulty as they objected strongly to harness and bridles. He eventually succeeded in driving a four-in-hand with three zebras and one pony down Piccadilly to Buckingham Palace. In later years a zebra fatally injured a groom.
Valerie Lapthorne, Aylesbury, Bucks.

☐ SOME years ago I used to stay at the Gwaai River Hotel in Western Zimbabwe. A seemingly tame zebra wandered the grounds. The manageress said it belonged to one of her African workers who regularly rode it like a horse. She showed me a cutting from a Bulawayo newspaper which showed him in action and the caption said that riding a zebra was unheard of. I spend much time bicycling through the African savannah where the typical village tractor always seems to be out of action awaiting some vital spare. A draught animal would be far more reliable. Villagers tell me that no zebra can be trained to do the job but they never give a reason or any evidence of anyone having tried to use the animal for this purpose.
Brian P. Moss, Kingsbury, Warwickshire.

☐ IN the 1984 movie, *Sheena*, Tanya Roberts as Queen of the Jungle is shown riding a zebra. This was in fact a horse painted black and white, as the ankles on zebras are too weak to carry a human being and would break. I therefore assume no one does ride them, as it would be nearly as cruel as making someone sit through *Sheena*.
Bill Reiss, London NW3.

☐ I WAS told by my father in the 1930s that a Mr Gaulstaun of Calcutta, who was a wealthy businessman and owned a string of racehorses, but unfortunately never won a famous race, once entered a male zebra for the Viceroy's Gold Cup, at the Royal Calcutta Turf Club. Of course, he had the zebra dyed black to resemble a horse. The zebra romped home by three necks. Mr Gaultaun's wife received the cup from the Vicereine, amid acclamation. But, sad to say, this being August – the monsoon period – the heavens opened up and the trick was revealed.

E. S. Arratoon, Tooting, London SW7.

☐ IN HIS book, *The Points of the Horse* (London, 1893), Captain M. Horace Hayes records that during one of his horse-breaking performances in South Africa he was able to persuade a young Burchell's zebra (*Equus burchelli*) to carry a rider on its back after an hour's gentle handling. A year earlier, in Calcutta, he had managed to saddle up an old true, or mountain zebra (*Equus hippotigris* – though Hayes gives it the nomenclature *Equus zebra*) belonging to a circus, but found it difficult to control: 'The reason being that the zebra's neck was so stiff and strong that I was unable to bend it in any direction [by use of the reins]. I soon taught it to do what I wanted in the circus; but when I rode it outside, it took me wherever it liked.' Burchell's zebra is taller than the true zebra and has a longer and suppler neck; in addition, its back tendons and suspensory ligaments are stronger, and 'much more like those of a well-bred horse than are those of the mountain zebra'. It was possibly three zebra of the Burchell type that Walter Rothschild used to drive his carriage. The African villagers referred to above may have been referring to the true zebra when said that zebras were intractable. Capt Hayes predicted that the Burchell zebra would one day be domesticated since it bred well in confinement, was easy to train and – unlike the true horse – was immune to the bite of the tsetse fly. That his prediction has not come true may be due more to the development of the internal combustion engine than to any deficiencies in the animal itself.

Peter Hazeldine, Todmorden, W Yorks.

☐ I ENCLOSE a photograph (above) from P Hill Beard's excellent book, *The End of the Game* (Hamlyn, 1965) showing Dr Rosendo Ribeiro, Nairobi's first doctor 'making his rounds' on a zebra. It suggests that despite some previous correspondents' submissions, a zebra can be ridden like a horse, and regularly.
Dick Tonkin, Pontcanna, Cardiff.

QUESTION: In *Three Men in a Boat*, J and Harris leave Waterloo by the 11.05 for Kingston (which had been the Exeter mail until they slipped the driver half a crown) from 'the high level platform'. Where is or was the high level platform?

☐ IN 1889, the year of *Three Men in a Boat*, Waterloo station was a rabbit-warren of a place and hard information about which platform was to be used for any particular departure was notoriously difficult to obtain. Jerome K. Jerome, wishing to make fun of this well-known situation, probably invented 'the high level platform' for comic effect: after all,

plenty of other stations, had such platforms. The only other possibility is that the author was referring erroneously to one of the four platforms at what is now known as Waterloo (East) on the Charing Cross to London Bridge line. Although this station once boasted a rail connection with the main Waterloo station, it was never used by either Exeter- or Kingston-bound trains.
Michael J. Smith, Southampton.

QUESTION: Are Scotch eggs really Scottish?

☐ THE practice of encasing a pre-cooked egg in forcemeat developed not in Scotland but in North Africa. The technique made its way Britain via France and was first recorded in England during the reign of Elizabeth I. Scotch eggs were originally spiked with cloves and highly spiced in an attempt to sweeten the often putrefying meat. The term itself is obscure but may come, though I doubt it, from a corruption of the word 'scorch' (which in Elizabethan times had ribald associations). The first Scotch eggs were cooked over a naked flame, after all. For more about Scotch eggs and Algerian cookery see Colin Cutler's excellent book, *1001 Strange Things* (Beaver Books, 1970).
Ali Mignot, London SW1.

☐ SCOTCH eggs originated in the Whitby area of Yorkshire in the late 19th century. Originally they were not covered in sausage meat but in a rich, creamy fish paste before being sprinkled with breadcrumbs. Their name in those days was 'Scotties', allegedly because they were made at an eatery by the name of William J Scott & Sons close to the seafront. Hence, over a period of time, the term Scotch eggs was adopted. This was thought to be because the major food-stores who started selling the delicacy were unhappy with the name and adopted a more formal approach to marketing. Sausage meat replaced the fish paste purely for packag-

ing ı-ısons, although on my last visit to Scarborough the original recipe was still being used in a local cafeteria. More information can be obtained from *Culinary Delights of Yorkshire* by Peter Bone (R. Fyfe & Co, 1981).
Robert Egan, Stevenage, Herts.

☐ ACCORDING to *A Caledonian Feast* by Annette Hope (Grafton Books, 1989), Scotch eggs were an Indian export in the early 19th century, along with curry and kedgeree. The dish was first mentioned by Meg Dods, circa 1830, in one of her recipe collections. Annette Hope continues: 'It bears an odd similarity – striking though probably coincidental – with an Indian dish called nargis kofta, which consists of hard-boiled eggs coated with cooked spiced minced mutton and fried, then cut in half and served in a sauce of curried tomato and onion' (p. 251).
Lynda Bowen, Nottingham.

QUESTION: What is the miracle ingredient which makes contact lens cleaning fluid so expensive (£3 for 30ml = £57 per pint = £455 per gallon)? Is there an effective alternative?

☐ PERHAPS it's a heavy dilution of the miracle ingredient in Elizabeth Arden's Millennium Night Cream which retails at £47.50 for 50ml (= £539.60 per pint = £4,316.80 per gallon).
A Mundy, Chingford, Essex.

☐ AND why is it sold in bottles containing enough to clean two lenses daily for three months with the instruction 'Dispose of unused contents within 28 days of opening'? I don't have six eyes.
Robert Hort, Bridgwater, Somerset.

☐ I HAVE worn hard lenses for 23 years, the last two pairs for

seven years each, and was complimented each time I changed them on their relatively unscratched condition. My method? To soak: tap water. To clean: spit. And the golden rule: never polish.
Averill M. Laing, Ashtead, Surrey.

□ A LITTLE Johnson's Baby Shampoo keeps my gas-permeable lenses shiny.
Lucia Costanzo, Brockley, London SE4.

□ FAIRY Liquid works well as a cleaner of grease from contact lenses (hard) and plain water for everyday. These tips were given to me at an optician's. I have used them successfully for years, thus saving pounds. Also, I occasionally use a sterilising tablet (about six a year).
(Ms) B. Hutchinson, Caine, Wilts.

□ I CANNOT explain why the fluids are so expensive; perhaps it is connected with the fact that most solutions are produced by two manufacturers. Fairy Liquid and baby shampoo may work well with obsolete hard lenses but may not be as compatible with the newest gas-permeable lens materials and certainly are not compatible with soft lenses. It is positively dangerous to use spit to clean contact lenses as many potentially sight-threatening micro-organisms inhabit the mouth. The purpose of soaking the lenses overnight is two-fold: (1) disinfection and (2) to keep the lens surface in a state in which it is easily wetted with tears. Tap water may meet requirement (2) but it certainly does not perform duty (1). Like spit, tap water contains many micro-organisms, some of which can cause corneal ulcers which are not only excruciatingly painful but also sight-threatening.
A. J. Elder Smith, MSc, MBCO, DCLP, Harrogate.

□ THE 'miracle ingredient' is sterility. Contact lens solutions are supplied sterile, in sterile containers, and are governed by the Medicines Act. These products all require a 'product licence' before they can be sold in the UK. Product licences take up to six years to develop and require continuing safety tests after the licence is granted. Licensing takes time and money. The Department of Health Medicines Control Agency licence fees have already risen from £8,000 for a Section 104 licence in November 1989 to £13,600 in February 1990. A forecast has been given for a further rise to £20,000 from December 1, 1990 and further, as yet unspecified, increases from April 1, 1991. These government-imposed costs cannot be absorbed by the manufacturers alone.

Elizabeth Smith, Association of Contact Lens Manufacturers Ltd, Camberley, Surrey.

QUESTION: 'A frog he would a-wooing go'. Who are the frog, Anthony Rowley and Miss Mousey?

☐ IN THE *OXFORD Dictionary of Nursery Rhymes*, Iona and Peter Opie say that the song goes back to the 16th century, but that we have to wait until about 1809 for the modern version with the refrain mentioning Anthony Rowley and 'rowley, powley, gammon and spinach'. They add that a manuscript of about 1760 gives a different refrain, in pseudo-Italian gibberish. In the later version the frog sets off on his abortive wooing 'with an opera hat', and Mrs Mousey asks him to 'give us a song'. Like a true operatic tenor he declines, having a cold. The frog's unfortunate story suggests dandyish behaviour, even social presumption, which leads us to a parody listed by the Opies, an indecent satire that Tom D'Urfey published in 1714, called Great Lord Frog to Lady Mouse. Here, a reprobate grandee is after Lady Mouse's youngest daughter; but he has no tail, and she won't marry a man who 'wants that needful ornament'. The Opies question the identification of Rowley (in the later song) with Charles II, 'Old Rowley' nor would D'Urfey have had the Merry Monarch in mind, for he assuredly did not lack a tail. The only strong candidate must be the Italian poet and opera-librettist, Paolo Antonio Rolli (1687–1765), who came to London in 1715 and worked as the first theatre-poet-cum-stage director of the Italian opera company founded in London in 1719. He wrote good lyric poems and epigrams, but poor librettos. An intriguer, he became Handel's enemy and went over to serve the rival 'Opera of the Nobility' later on. His main income probably came from other activities: he taught Italian and singing to the wives and daughters of great families, among them the royal princesses. Several of his lyrics praise the charms of society ladies, some of them known to have been his pupils; several epigrams complain that beautiful Englishwomen will not marry poor men, particularly foreigners, and indeed he seems not to have married. He returned to Italy in 1744. The name Paolo Antonio Rolli, or in the Italian manner Rolli Paolo, gives us both 'Rowley-Powley' and 'Anthony Rowley-o'. 'Roly-poly' was at that time a kind of ball-game; it did not mean a jam-pudding until the 19th century, though the Opies suggest its use in dialect to mean a boiled chicken (whence, no doubt, the addition of 'gammon and spinach'). A London pamphlet satirising the Italian opera, published in 1734 and once attributed to Dr Arbuthnot, offers a spoof cantata text from the original Italian of that incomparable Dramatick Poet, Seignior 'Rowley-Powley' which can refer only to Rolli. Though contemporary gossip gives us no clue beyond a certain dislike of this self-ingratiating and over-paid foreigner, it seems likely enough that Rolli, a man living by his wits and very susceptible to feminine charms (as his poems suggest), must have overstepped the mark with a rich gentlewoman. Some wag would have recalled D'Urfey's application of the old song and decided to fit it out again for Rolli. That might account for the otherwise inexplicable 'opera hat' and the singing. I can't explain the marriage-broking Rat or Mrs Mousey, who like the Frog himself were already characters in the song.

Brian Trowell, Heather Professor of Music, Oxford University.

QUESTION: Who first coined the saying 'A camel is a horse designed by a committee'?

☐ I DON'T know, but I expect it was the same person who said 'An elephant is a mouse designed to government specifications'.
B. Palmer, Waterlooville, Hants.

☐ I HAVE no idea who first made a connection between camels and committees, but it seems to me to be used very unthinkingly. If the intention is to denigrate the work of committees, it does not support the case. A camel is a highly efficient machine for its function and not merely a misshapen horse.
Frank Jackson, Harlow, Essex.

☐ IT WAS Sir Alec Issigonis, the designer of the Mini car. According to a BBC television news report following his death last year, he coined the phrase to illustrate his dislike of working in teams.
Martin McDonald, Chorlton-cum-Hardy, Manchester.

QUESTION: During the Second World War children were encouraged to collect horse chestnuts (conkers) and contribute them to the war effort. Why?

☐ I WAS one of the children. At my school, we were regularly sent out on foraging parties, bringing back, in season, huge quantities of the things. Unfortunately, those in authority failed to tell us for what purpose we were gathering them. A rumour, growing ultimately into a certainty, spread among us, to the effect that they were used in making toothpaste,

presumably because the ingredients for real toothpaste were scarce or unobtainable. To this day, every time I brush my teeth, I devoutly believe that I am using, by some alchemy, essence of conker.
Bernard Levin, London W1.

☐ IT WAS in the belief, possibly mistaken, that conkers could be fed to pigs and thus increase the indigenous food supply. There was some connection, too, between this activity and the pig clubs that were allowed, by special government dispensation, to flourish in urban areas outside the scope of the wartime restrictions on the traditional agricultural industry. Under these arrangements, a number of citizens could band together, find suitable accommodation and acquire a piglet or two which could be fed on their collective household waste and eventually, slaughtered for distribution among the club members without penalty to their normal food rations. The pig clubs generated a tremendous amount of conspiratorial activity among their members, both in the search for any pigfood which could be acquired without promising favours to outsiders when the pigs were killed, and in the competition with other clubs over the quantity and quality of the pork ultimately produced. All wartime life was there – including, possibly, disinformation.
Peter M. Scott, Fleet, Hants.

☐ HORSE chestnuts were collected for the purpose of using their starch as a substitute for maize in a fermentation process to produce acetone. Acetone is a minute but essential ingredient in the manufacture of cordite, the principal propellant used in heavy artillery. The process for its manufacture from starch was pioneered during the First World War by the chemist, Chaim Weizmann, who is best remembered as a passionate Zionist and the first president of Israel.
Frank Egerton, Appley Bridge, Wigan.

QUESTION: Why does Mickey Mouse wear gloves? Are there any films in which he isn't wearing them?

□ WALT DISNEY was pushed into creating Mickey Mouse by the fact that he had just lost the rights to an earlier character, Oswald the Lucky Rabbit. Apart from the ears and tail the early Mickey is remarkably similar to Oswald and, like him, had no shoes and no gloves. In *Plane Crazy*, made as a silent film in 1928 and released later with sound, Mickey is barefooted and barehanded. *Gallopin' Gaucho* (again silent, 1928) sees Mickey in shoes for the first time and he kept them on for *Steamboat Willie*. The gloves came, I think, with either *The Barn Dance* (1928) or *The Opry House* (1929). As for the gloves, here's an explanation from Walt himself: 'We didn't want him to have mouse hands, because he was supposed to be more human. So we gave him gloves. Five Fingers looked like too much on such a little figure, so we took one away. That was just one less finger to animate.' A very down-to-earth approach. And if you put gloves on a cartoon character, you don't have to animate all those wrinkles and lines. Incidentally, there's a similar evolutionary path that can be traced to the emergence of Bugs

Bunny's gloves in *A Wild Hare*, Tex Avery's 1940 cartoon
that gave us the classic phrase, 'What's Up Doc?'
Rolf Harris, Rolf's Cartoon Club, HTV West, Bristol.

**QUESTION: The familiar Christmas crib with the ani-
mals is not in the Christian canon. Can anyone say
which apocryphal gospel, rejected by the Church, it
came from and why the Church sanctions its use?**

☐ THE Christmas crib does originate in the canonical New
Testament, in St Luke's Gospel, ch 2, vv 7, 12, and 16 (cf, St
Matthew ch 2 v 11). It can be inferred from the use of a
manger as a cradle for the baby that the family was accommodated in the stable or cattleshed attached to the inn. This
arrangement of buildings was very common in the Middle
East in the Roman period — and even today. It is likely that
the building was a stable rather than a cattleshed, because
travellers using inns needed somewhere to tether and feed
their pack-animals. In the Greek it says there was not a
topos (place, seat, space) in the inn itself, where a woman
could give birth. There might have been a private room for
distinguished guests, and others could gather round the fire
in the open courtyard. The whole scene must have been a
familiar one on the great highways of the Roman provinces,
as the merchants, couriers and refugees vied for places in the
caravanserai.
J. M. Frayn, Kingston-on-Thames, Surrey.

☐ THE *Apocryphal New Testament* by M Rhodes James
gives extracts (page 75) from the *Liber de Infantica* which
he describes as 'the Gospel of pseudo-Matthew', stating that
dragons, lions, leopards and wolves came to join the oxen
and sheep brought by Mary and Joseph to the stable. The
point, presumably, is that because the oxen and sheep were
not devoured a prophecy of Isaiah was fulfilled. This gospel
is thought to originate in the 8th century; but the earliest

existing manuscript is of the 11th century. The idea appears to have been accepted by the Church through St Francis making a model of the crib with ox and ass in 1223 after gaining the approval of Honorius III who saw the crib when he visited Greccio on Christmas Eve, 1224.
Robert Sephton, Oxford.

☐ REMEMBERING that the 'three kings' or Magi did not come until later, the figures and animals of the Christmas crib as assembled have no relationship to events but strangely are symbolic and are best related to the Jewish Kabbalah, a system said to have been taught in Capernaum around 500 BC, although not really known in the west until the Middle Ages. The three kings with their three gifts of gold, frankincense and myrrh, the father, mother and child, the shepherds and angels, the ass and the ox are all symbols related in their turn to the Kabbalah tree which also gives us the phrase 'Thine is the Kingdom, the Power and the Glory'. The animals represent the Kingdom on Earth: the ox is the animal of the plough, while the ass is the animal of the journey, the spiritual journey.
(Mrs) Greta James, Shaftesbury, Dorset.

QUESTION: Why does one never see baby pigeons?

☐ ANYONE who has seen a young pigeon, or squab to give it its correct name, will not wish to see another. They are extremely fat, fed as they are on rich milk; the beginnings of their feathers are so waxy that they not only feel almost slimy, but flakes of it cover their bodies to give the impression of incurable psoriasis. They are also extremely ugly, bearing an uncanny resemblance to a former ancestor of theirs, the dodo, as they sit squirming in their nests.
Mick Allen, Brighton.

☐ THIS year, despite great efforts to discourage them,

pigeons decided to 'nest' on my balcony. We live on the 21st floor. Two eggs were laid in the drain hole – there was no nest. Both parents sat on the eggs and seemed to change over every four hours. Eventually the eggs hatched and to my amazement the chicks were bright yellow – quite pretty in fact. The parents cared for them marvellously. For hours one would stand with outstretched wings to shade them from the sun while the other brought food. This wonderful display of parental devotion was maintained until the babies were as big as their parents and had the same appearance. When they flew away one could not distinguish the babies from the adults.
Eileen Brennan, London W10.

☐ I THINK the questioner may be talking about feral pigeons which, by the time they leave the nest at about five weeks old, are fully feathered and about two-thirds the size of their parents. They are easily distinguishable to the trained eye. Two points one may look out for in young pigeons are the lack of 'wattles' above the nose (which grow quite large on adult birds) and also the size of the 'cere' (white outer ring of the eye), which is also larger on adults.
T. W. Lynn, Chopwell, Newcastle-upon-Tyne.

QUESTION: Where does the saying to 'pour oil on troubled waters' come from?

☐ OIL lowers the surface tension of water, leaving it with a weaker 'skin'. This decreases its ability to form peaks and waves.
Joy Bampton, London SE16.

☐ AS A YOUNG Merchant Navy deck hand, preparing to become an AB, I had to learn about the lifeboat's stores and equipment. Among the strange-sounding items listed in my *Seamanship Handbook* (published 1952) were *gripes, lazy*

painters, becketed grab lines and 'a supply of one gallon of vegetable, fish or animal oil and an appliance for distributing the oil easily on the water, arranged for attachment to the sea anchor'. The book explains: 'A very small quantity of oil, skilfully applied, may prevent damage, both to ships (especially the smaller classes) and to boats, by modifying the action of breaking seas . . . The thickest oils are most effectual. Refined kerosene is of little use; crude petroleum is serviceable when nothing else is obtainable; but all animal and vegetable oils, such as waste oils from the engine, have great effect. The best method of application in a ship at sea appears to be: hanging over the side, in such a manner as to be in the water, small canvas bags, capable of holding from one to two gallons of oil, such bags being pricked with a sail needle to facilitate leakage of the oil.'
Peter Mungall, Education Officer, RRS Discovery, *Dundee.*

☐ In his *Ecclesiastical History* of AD 731 the Venerable Bede writes that St Aidan gave a priest who was about to set out on a sea journey a cruse of oil, saying to him, 'Remember to throw into the sea the oil which I give you, when straightaway the winds will abate, and a calm and smiling sea will accompany you throughout your voyage.'
(Rev) Kenneth Chambers, Heathfield, E Sussex.

☐ Benjamin Franklin was fond of performing a conjuring trick to illustrate this. Leading a friend out to a pond on a windy day he would lower the knob of his walking stick into the water, muttering abracadabra-type incantations. Almost at once the surface would become eerily calm. After a moment the astonished spectator would be treated to an explanation: Franklin's rod was hollow and contained a reservoir of oil. It's a great trick; I've tried it and it produces an ovation every time.
Tom Cutler, Hove, E. Sussex.

QUESTION: Who tested the first parachute and did he live to tell the tale?

☐ DISREGARDING Chinese acrobats who, in order to entertain the emperor in the 16th century, were supposed to have jumped from various heights with umbrellas attached to themselves, and Fausto Veranzio of Venice who is supposed to have tested a crude form of parachute in 1616, it is generally accepted that Sebastian le Normand of Montpellier in France was the first person to test a parachute. This he did on Boxing Day in 1783, jumping from the tower of Montpellier Observatory, attached to a rigid parachute made of canvas and wicker-work. He landed safely. Balloonists developed and refined this form of rigid parachute and made numerous descents, with varying degrees of success, as part of the general entertainment associated with ballooning. The originator of the folded parachute, capable of being stored in a container and opening on descent, was Major Thomas Baldwin of the US who, in 1850, began successful demonstrations of his equipment, again by dropping from a balloon. However, the parachutes suffered from the limitation that they were attached to the balloon and were only opened by means of the parachutist dropping away, pulling the parachute from its container and, when fully extended, breaking the cord attaching the parachute to the balloon. The reputed inventor of the self-contained manually opened parachute capable of being worn about a person's body was Leo Stevens of the US who, in 1908, is said to have demonstrated such a parachute, though it was not until the First World War that such parachutes became generally available.
Steve Day, Salisbury, Wilts.

QUESTION: How many British governments have been elected with over 50 per cent of the votes cast (say since 1900)?

☐ FOUR. In 1900 the Conservative Government was returned with 51 per cent of the votes cast; Lloyd George's coupon election in 1918 secured 69 per cent for coalition candidates; the National Government was returned in 1931 and again in 1935 with 67 per cent and 54 per cent respectively. Otherwise, the nearest a prime minister has got to receiving a majority of the votes cast was Eden in 1955, with just under 50 per cent. By contrast, the best that Mrs Thatcher was able to achieve was just over 42 per cent in 1983, which was rewarded under our unfair electoral system with a Commons majority of 144 seats.
Rodney Brazier, Reader in Constitutional Law, University of Manchester.

QUESTION: In a Christmas cracker my mother found the conundrum 'Why is a mouse when it spins?' The answer was given as 'Because the higher the fewer.' Is there any meaning to this?

☐ THIS 'nonsense' question was popular among the RAF apprentices at Halton, Bucks, in the early 1950s, when the full version was: 'Why is a mouse when it spins? Because the higher they fly the fewer, and the engine driver's name was Smith. Why was his name Smith? Because his father's name was Smith.' Apart from the logic of the last bit, the repartee had no meaning whatsoever and was probably the precursor of the Monty Python type of humour.
John Nixon, Horley, Surrey.

☐ THE CORRECT wording should have been 'Why *does* a mouse when it spins?' with the then obvious answer 'Higher or lower'. At least that was the version which sixth formers

at Quarry Bank High School in Liverpool used in the early 1960s to test the gullibility of younger members of the school such as myself. It was rumoured that it had been devised by John Lennon, a pupil at the school until 1959, but perhaps I am being gullible in believing this.
Geoff Black, Cambridge.

☐ 1919. The Black and Tans were prodding the armchairs with bayonets to see if the stuffing was hand-grenades. We kids were lined against the wall. 'When is your husband expected?' the officer asked my mother. 'When is a mouse when she spins?' she replied, adding, to his elevated eyebrows, 'The higher the fewer'. He and we knew the conversation was closed. He gathered his men and left – without finding the wireless transmitter under the aspidistra.
Maurice F. deCogan, Dalkey, Co Dublin.

☐ THE RIDDLE first came to my attention as a student fresher in 1942. At the same time another phrase was popular. In answer to any question to which one could give no answer, such as 'Have you seen so-and-so?' or 'Have you read such-and-such?' the reply would be 'No, but my sister rides a bicycle.' There was also a sort of son-of-mouse to which the answer was 'No, but you can clean a straw hat with a lemon.' Unfortunately I've forgotten the question. Although this appears to be so much student nonsense, it taught me the meaning of *non sequitur*. As Hugh Lloyd said to Tony Hancock in *The Blood Donor*, 'For things unknown there is no knowing.'
Peter M. Horsey MA, Stockbury, Sittingbourne, Kent.

☐ BRUNEL again (he was a boyhood hero of mine). This peculiar saying relates to a certain type of governor on steam engines, whereby revolutions of the engine are reduced if a spinning weight (mouse) is lifted up a shaft by its centrifugal force, releasing steam pressure and ensuring fewer revs: the higher, the fewer. Such systems were common on static

engines like those found originally in cotton mills in the heyday of the steam revolution.
Patrick Nethercot, Durham.

QUESTION: Who is the BBC2 test card girl, and what has happened to her?

□ WHEN the BBC were planning the test card in 1967, it was decided to have a child, because her clothes and hairstyle would be less likely to date. When professional models proved unsuitable, a BBC engineer suggested his daughter, and Carol Hersee, eight years old, became 'The Most Seen Girl on TV' – a special award given by Pye in 1971. She became a seamstress at Berman's, the theatrical costumiers, and subsequently worked in the wardrobe department at Shepperton studios.
Norman Brindley, St Albans, Herts.

QUESTION: What is the origin of 'Lloyd George knew my father'?

□ THE ORIGINAL version was more pointed: 'Lloyd George knew my mother.' The substitution of 'father' seems to have been made in interests of discretion and delicacy, but I have no idea when or by whom this splendid old chant was bowdlerised.
Alan Cock, Southampton.

□ I HAVE long believed that this is a corruption of 'Lloyd George Knows My Father' – a derisive ditty sung by First World War soldiers in the days of conscription when out marching and passing a man in civvies but apparently of military age. But I cannot verify it.
(Dr) Henry Pelling, St John's College, Cambridge.

☐ ALAN COCK and Henry Pelling may be correct, but the song was also a satirical reference to the way Lloyd George's government handed out honours, and especially peerages, with little restraint. Liberally, indeed.
T. Mason, Halifax, W Yorks.

☐ THERE is a snag in T. Mason's proposal. To obtain an honour, one did not need to make personal contact with Lloyd George: one simply sent a cheque for the amount indicated in the 'price list', to his patronage agent, Maundy Gregory. Nowadays, of course, we have more civilised ways of distributing honours. If you are head of a large company, simply arrange for your company (not yourself) to contribute liberally to Tory party funds. (Alas, you have to become big in business in the first place!). An easier route is by securing a safe Tory seat in Parliament.
Alan Cook, Southampton.

QUESTION: Why is the sea salty?

☐ WEATHERING and erosion of the minerals of the earth's surface release many ions to be washed into the seas. The main ones are iron, magnesium, potassium, calcium carbonate, sulphate, chlorine and sodium. All except the last two are readily involved in organic and chemical reactions, yielding new sedimentary rocks. Sodium and chlorine therefore have built up as a residue throughout geological time, and indeed the salinity of the sea has been used as a basis of measuring the age of the ocean.
E. J. Marsden (retired teacher of geology), Stockport.

☐ THE REAL puzzle about the sea is why it is not more salty. It is a relatively simple matter to measure the rate at which sodium chloride is carried to the sea by rivers and then calculate how quickly the concentration of salts builds up. These estimates indicate that it would take only a few hundred million years for the sea to become a completely saturated sodium chloride solution – yet the sea at present is well below saturation point. Furthermore, palaeontological evidence seems to show that the concentration of the sea stays relatively constant. Where has all the excess sodium chloride been going over four billion years of earth history? How is it returned to the land, or lost into the earth's crust? Human and biological activity has negligible effect. Some salt is removed at ocean ridge hot springs, and this process accounts for the balance in concentration of salts of other elements (iron, magnesium, etc) but does not remove nearly enough sodium chloride to explain why the sea is not saturated. Is anyone able to throw any more light on this problem?

Thomas Chapman, King's College, Cambridge.

QUESTION: Shoe shops in the 1950s had X-ray type machines for customers to check the fit of their shoes. How did these work, and were they harmful?

□ THESE MACHINES, known in this country by their trade name, Pedoscope, were indeed X-ray machines, of a specialised type called fluoroscopes. In these, the X-ray image is made visible by a fluorescent screen rather than on photographic film. The screen comprises a layer of crystals of barium platinocyanide (or similar substance) which have the property of emitting a green light under the influence of X-rays. This image is naturally rather faint, so Pedoscopes incorporated a viewing tube into which customers gazed to see the bones of their feet and the nails in their shoes. Other types of fluoroscope were commonly used for chest screening. Concern about pedoscopes was first expressed in this country in 1950, and the Home Office issued guidelines in 1958, requiring control of the length and intensity of doses, the training of staff, and the display of health warnings. Some felt that harm outweighed usefulness and that the practice should be discontinued. The concern was that there was no control over the number of exposures the public, and children in particular, might undergo. Shop staff might also be at risk from scattered radiation or, in one reported case, from demonstrating the apparatus to customers. All fluoroscopes gave a larger radiation dose than contemporary film X-rays because the exposure was longer to allow viewing and the X-ray source more intense to create a sufficiently bright image. The Science Museum has a Pedoscope in its reserve collections.

Timothy Boon, Science Museum, London SW7.

☐ IN THE early 1950s I worked for a well-known firm of shoe shops. Each workday for a couple of years I operated a Pedoscope. This machine allowed one to see the position of the foot in relation to the shoe the customer wished to purchase. A foot was placed in a slot at the base of the machine and the assistant viewed the X-ray through a screen at the top. Suddenly, over a short period, the machines were jettisoned by the firm – some actually being destroyed on the premises. Something was wrong! How radically wrong I was to become only too well aware. Twenty-five years later I developed a cancerous tumour which necessitated the removal of my right lung. Thankfully the expertise and care I was given saved my life but left me a partial invalid. My doctor assured me that the tumour was not caused by smoking – I knew that for I had never smoked or worked and lived in a smokey environment. The *Encyclopaedia Britannica* lists the use of Pedoscopes as a dangerous occupation. There was no other reason for the development of the tumour except through the prolonged use of the Pedoscope. It was a great pity that the firm I had worked for did not monitor its workers in its shops after its hasty decision to withdraw the machines. Perhaps other people have also suffered from the same experience.

Dorothy Simpson, Burnley, Lancs.

QUESTION: Why are people hanged but pictures hung?

☐ THERE are two verbs 'to hang': (1) intransitive, with the irregular past participle 'hung,' derived from the Anglo Saxon hangian, corresponding to the intransitive German hangen, which also has the irregular past participle gehangen. So we say 'I hang on the gibbet' (present) and 'I hung on the gibbet' (past); and (2) transitive, with the regular past participle 'hanged', derived from the Old Norse hanga, corresponding to the transitive German hangen, which has the regular past participle gehangt. So we say 'I hang you on the gibbet' (present) and 'I hanged you on the gibbet' (past). 'He was hanged' is the passive voice of '(someone) hanged him,' i.e., of the transitive verb and is correct. 'He was hung' is wrong but 'He hung (on the gibbet)' is OK. '(The decorations) were hanged on the Christmas tree' is correct but pedantic: '. . . were hung . . .' would sound correct nowadays but is wrong; '. . . hung . . .' is correct but means something different. Shakespeare put it more simply, but incorrectly: 'Beef, sir, is hung, men are hanged.'
C. J. Squire, Twickenham.

☐ I'M HANGED if I agree completely with C. J. Squire. He is right up to a point. In modern English, the irregular (strong) form of the verb 'to hang' is equally correct, whether used transitively or intransitively. The regular (weak) form – 'hanged' (past tense and past participle) – is archaic except when used to describe capital punishment.
Brian Davenport, Blackburn, Lancs.

☐ C. J. SQUIRE gives the impression of not knowing the difference between a past participle and the past tense. He tells us the past participle 'hung' is derived from the Anglo-Saxon 'hangian', which in itself is difficult to see, and then he proceeds to give an example of the use of this past participle, 'I hung on the gibbet', rather than 'I have hung on the gibbet'. His examples, anyway, are ludicrous. Has

anyone ever had occasion to say 'I hang on the gibbet', 'I hung on the gibbet', 'I hang you on the gibbet', or 'I hanged you on the gibbet'? If C. J. Squire is a teacher of languages (heaven forbid!), I hope he will manage to give more useful examples.
(Mrs) M. M. Varley, Lutterworth, Leics.

☐ THREE categories of people are hung: juries, parliaments and male Americans (either well or badly).
Peter Mellor, City University, London EC1.

QUESTION: When were elastic bands invented, and by whom?

☐ THE FIRST elastic bands, made from vulcanised rubber, were patented on March 17, 1845, by Stephen Perry of Messrs Perry & Co, rubber manufacturers of London. Production of rubber bands 'for papers, letters, etc' was inaugurated by the firm at about the same time.
Sean Tyler, Orpington, Kent.

☐ THE ENGLISHMAN Thomas Hancock invented the rubber band in about 1820. The bands invented at that time were not vulcanised and would soften on hot days or harden on cold ones. The American Charles Goodyear invented vulcanisation in the 1840s, but Hancock was quick to exploit the technique (and claimed the invention!): vulcanisation eliminated the temperature dependence of rubber behaviour.
K. P. Jones, The Malaysian Rubber Producers' Research Association, Tun Abdul Razak Laboratory, Brickendonbury, Herts.

☐ ELASTIC BANDS evolved by chance in the rubber plantations of the Congo (now Zaire) as long ago as the last century. Felix Saabye, director of the Canada India Rubber Company, noticed his labourers working raw latex between their fingers until it became firm and elastic. They wore long bands of this substance around their heads as ornament. Saabye used these flexible bands around company documents in place of the usual cloth tape. Unfortunately the raw latex was unstable and quickly broke down but Saabye found that when he dusted the rubber with kaolin it would last longer without sticking to itself. Saabye was unable to interest backers in his 'Indiarubber tape' however, and the idea died with him. The development of high temperature sulphur vulcanisation led eventually to the modern production of long, extruded tubes still dusted with powder which are subsequently cut into the durable elastic bands most people know today. My company is presently undertaking research to combat the short life of rubber bands in hot places like Los Angeles where I have a hard time with the darn things breaking down.

Harvey Weintraub, Chairman, National Latex, McLean, Virginia, US.

QUESTION: Why is depression the 'blues'? Why is a coward 'yellow'? Why is one 'green' with envy?

☐ ASSIGNING colours to moods is tied in with Eastern philosophies, and the idea that the body emanates an aura of light, made up of the colour spectrum. Some mystics are able to see or sense these auras as colours, and are able to measure strengths and deficiencies in the areas assigned to each colour. These areas, or chakras, are defined as follows: red indicating sexuality or reproduction (and the basic emotion, anger); orange for the digestive system and expresses physical energy; yellow for the solar plexus area; green for the heart; blue in the throat and shoulders; indigo in the forehead (where lies intuition and healing); and violet in the crown of the head (for appreciation and creativity). Colour therapy, meditation and yoga are some of the alter-

native ways of actively promoting good health by concentrating on certain chakras. To answer the specific questions feeling 'blue' signifies a need to encourage the blue chakra (depression and the inability to communicate are symptoms of a malfunctioning thyroid gland which lies in the throat area). 'Cowardice', fear or lack of purpose shows a need to energise the yellow centre; 'contemplating one's navel' or focusing the mind's eye on this area promotes a sense of self-worth. The 'green envy' might be explained as a lack of love and respect for others. When all the colours are strongly balanced, the person is said to possess a strong 'spectral' light, or has 'attained enlightenment'. The study of colours can provide an insight on everyday phenomena: how we choose to decorate ourselves and our surroundings, Van Gogh's paintings, even politics. Do 'blue Tories' lack joy and honest communication, is 'red Labour' motivated by anger, and are 'yellow Liberals' afflicted by a sense of purposelessness? The continued and appropriate use of colourful expressions is evidence founded, not on scientific knowledge, but on instinctive biophilic awareness.
S. Dudley, Sheffield, S. Yorks.

☐ I CAME across the following in an 1856 edition of *Chambers's Journal* (Saturday, July 12, 1856; no 132): 'In an article in the *Journal of Psychological Medicine* on Baron Feuchtersleben's *Principles of Medical Psychology* showing how the mind is influenced by a mechanical calling, there is this curious sentence: Rosch and Esquirol confirm from observation that indigo-dyers become melancholy; and those who dye scarlet choleric. Their observation regarding indigo-dyers affords a strong confirmation of the statement of that arch-quack, Paracelsus, who declared blue to be injurious. This would seem to suggest that our phrase "the blue devils" may derive from a scientific fact.'
Adam Roberts, Southampton.

☐ I BELIEVE there is scientific proof of an association of mood with colour among the higher primates. Some years ago I was involved in the rehabilitation of a group of infant chimpanzees which had been confiscated from illegal dealers. The young chimps were being held in rather dreary surroundings before being moved to a rehabilitation camp in the forest, and I devised a series of behavioural tests, as much to keep the chimps from being bored as to advance scientific knowledge. Among these tests was one on colour preferences: wooden blocks, painted in a variety of colours, were put in front of the young chimps, and their choices were noted. Initially, the results were what would be expected from human children: a preference for bright primary colours. But when results were correlated with other factors, some interesting results were forthcoming. We noted colour choices in relation to weather (dull, cool, rainy days/bright sunny days) hunger (before feeding time when the subjects were hungry/after feeding), and companionship (tests done by an individual separated from the group/ together with the group). All the negative factors (poor weather/hunger/loneliness) elicited a shift towards colour choices in which blues, as well as grey, brown and black predominated. On the other hand, positive factors (sunny weather/good food/companionship) shifted the colour choices towards reds, yellows and bright green. It was interesting to note that during this period, one of the group died. She had been maltreated by the person from whom she was confiscated, and was the weakling of the group. On the day of her death, all the other chimps chose dull, subdued colours. It was also interesting that the male self-appointed leader of the group always sought, by pushing and elbowing, to grab the most favoured colour, but was often outwitted by the eldest female. All surviving subjects of these tests have returned to their forest home and so far as we can tell, have integrated with the wild.

V A Sackey, Accra, Ghana.

QUESTION: How are words inserted into sticks of (e.g. Blackpool) rock? Where and when did this promotional ploy originate?

☐ A DISTANT ancestor of mine was a partner in the sweet-making firm of Slade & Bullock. 'The Bullock' of the partnership was Ben Bullock, a Burnley miner who moved to Dewsbury in 1868 and began selling boiled sweets in Dewsbury and Heckmondwike markets. In 1876 he formed his own company and began increasing his range of products. One of these new products was the first example of lettered rock. I continue the story by quoting from an article in the *Dewsbury Reporter*, published in 1976. 'Ben turned out his first batch of lettered rock with the words "Whoa Emma" inside them as a tribute to a popular song of the day. The Whoa Emma rock sold like magic at West Riding markets but bigger things were yet to come. 'The discovery of a paper which could cover the sticks of rock and yet be removed easily coincided with Ben's decision to take a fortnight's holiday at the home of Mr John Pilling, of Talbot Street Post Office, Blackpool. Shortly afterwards a few hundredweight of Blackpool lettered rock was sent to the resort and the novelty so caught the public fancy that the Dewsbury firm was inundated with orders from seaside resorts all over Britain. [Ben Bullock's] fame spread abroad and demands for lettered rock arrived from all over the world, with exports going to such places as Malta, the Sudan, India and Australia.' Unfortunately I can't answer the first half of the question; there's nothing in my family archive to tell how the trick was done.
J. E. Slade, New Malden, Surrey.

☐ A STORY that most students of sociology come across at some time and which never fails to amuse can be found in a report by Taylor & Walton, entitled *Industrial Sabotage: Motives & Meanings* (1971). 'They had to throw away half a mile of Blackpool rock last year, for, instead of the custom-

ary motif running through its length, it carried the terse injunction "F– – – OFF". A worker dismissed by a sweet factory had effectively demonstrated his annoyance by sabotaging the product of his labour.'
Anthony Ward, Cheadle Hulme, Cheshire.

☐ IN 1956, as a teenager wanting to earn money for a trip to Belgium, I worked long hot hours at Jimmy Rowlands's Rock Shop in High Street, Folkestone. There the rock-makers took thick strips of still-hot red rock and laid them in square shapes (like modern digital figures on a video recorder or watch) so that the letter F for Folkestone was built up using one vertical and two horizontal bars of different sizes. In between the red strips, white rock was used as a spacer, and stainless steel bars kept the letters together until they were wrapped in a coating of white rock and covered in red. The resulting large lump, when rolled and stretched, gradually became the size of the normal stick of rock, and was then chopped into appropriate sizes and allowed to cool.
Mary M. Redman, Writtle, Essex.

☐ THE ORIGIN of lettered rock has been claimed by Black-pool's smaller neighbour and would-be rival, Morecambe. The town's claim is not easy to prove. In his recent history of the town – *Lost Resort? The Flow and Ebb of Morecambe* (Cicerone Press, 1990) – Roger Bingham repeats the claim. But even in such a closely-researched book, the most he can conclude is that 'though other resorts have challenged the claim that seaside rock originated in Morecambe, lettered rock probably did' (p. 184). On the same page, there is a picture of Dick Taylor's rock shop and Mr Bingham dates the production of the first lettered rock to 'about 1925'.
Lester Mather, Kendal, Cumbria.

QUESTION: Considering the disgusting substances investigated very closely by dogs, are there any odours they find repellent?

☐ MY retriever backs off with horror from disinfectant, Vick vapour rub and peppermint essence. She's not keen on mothballs, either.
Julia Sutherland, Teddington, Middlesex.

☐ THEY will run off if approached with a slice of lemon.
Maria Scott, London SE5.

☐ OUR dog dislikes the smell of whisky. She will back off sharply if the aroma comes within six inches of her nose. But I don't complain; her loss is my gain.
Simon Cobby, Cambridge.

QUESTION: Why are colourful patterns seen when one rubs one's eyes in the dark?

☐ THIS IS caused by the light receptors in the eye being stimulated mechanically when the eyes are rubbed rather

than by their usual stimulant, light. The brain interprets the signal sent from the eyes as a coloured flash. This phenomenon is one of a number known as photopsia – the awareness of a flash of light without an apparent external cause.
Andrew Morgan, Kiddlington, Oxon.

QUESTION: Shostakovich wrote a classic arrangement of 'Tea for Two'. Why did he call it 'Tahiti Trot'?

☐ SHOSTAKOVICH orchestrated 'Tea for Two' in 45 minutes in 1927, to win a bet with Nicolai Malko, the conductor. Malko performed the orchestration to great public acclaim in Moscow and Leningrad. Later, it became part of Shostakovich's first ballet, *The Golden Age*. In 1929, the Central Committee of the Bolshevik Party called a conference of musicians to discuss the 'foxtrotting problem'; foxtrots were henceforth officially disapproved of as products of the decadent and hedonistic West. 'Tea for Two' was officially 'renamed' 'Tahiti Trot', presumably in order to emphasise its Western character and the very fact that it was a foxtrot. Shostakovich was forced, against his inclinations, to write a letter to *The Proletarian Musician*, expressing his distaste for music in the 'light genre'. The concert arrangement was withdrawn and the ballet quickly fell out of the repertoire; it is only recently that the arrangement has been rediscovered and performed.
Michael Downes, King's College, Cambridge.

QUESTION: What is the derivation of the term 'round robin'?

☐ AN EARLY use of the term was aboard 18th-century ships. Conditions were often very bad, and crews were known to mutiny. Sometimes this would take the form of a petition to the captain asking for better treatment. The usual reaction

of the captain was to look for the name at the top of the left-hand column, and hang him from the yardarm. To get round this, the crew would instead sign a 'round robin' in the shape of a circle. This, however, did not help much, because the captain would then take reprisals against the man whose name was in the 12 o'clock position (known as the 'ringleader'). Apart from the obvious alliteration, I do not know why it should be called a 'robin'.
Keith Trobridge, Shipley, W. Yorks.

☐ AN EARLIER use of the term was as a blasphemous name for the sacrament, c1555: 'There were at Paules fixed railing bils against the Sacrament, terming it Jacke of ye boxe, the sacrament of the halter, round Robin, with lyke unseemely termes.' (Ridley, quoted in *Oxford English Dictionary*).
Frank Cummins, Warley, W. Midlands.

QUESTION: In the story of *Goldilocks and the Three Bears,* why is it that Daddy Bear's porridge was too hot, Mummy Bear's porridge was too cold and yet Baby Bear's was 'just right'? These observations appear to place the temperature of the smallest portion between that of the largest and middle-sized portions. Is there some simple explanation of the anomalous cooling rates of the three bowls?

☐ IGNORING for a moment the insulating properties of the Bear family's breakfast porcelain, let's apply Newton's law of cooling. Heat loss varies as temperature difference (which at the start is the same for all three) multiplied by surface area. Rate of cooling varies as rate of heat loss divided by volume. Suppose that Baby Bear had half as much porridge as his mother and one-third as much as his father. In most families, adults use the same set of dishes while babies have their own smaller dishes, usually prettily decorated (Baby Bear's may have had pictures of cuddly little men on it).

Mummy's shallow pool of porridge cools more quickly than Daddy's deeper portion; as long as the radius of the adult dish is between 1.45 and 1.8 times that of Baby's dish, Baby's porridge will cool at a rate partway between that of his father and that of his mother. This is of course a simplified calculation. As different rates of cooling take effect, it becomes necessary to take temperature difference into account, involving the use of calculus. The insulating power of the dishes would also have to be allowed for, together with any difference in insulation between the two types of dish.

(Miss) C. A. Bryson, West Kirby, Merseyside.

☐ WHEN considering the problem, one must surely examine the character of the porridge thief herself. Given that Goldilocks has trespassed on the property of the three bears, and stolen their porridge, would we be correct to take her testimony concerning temperatures of the porridge at face value? I contest that it is simply wilful whim that causes her to eat the porridge of Baby Bear and the temperature argument is a smokescreen to divert attention from her theft. Why are our sympathies aroused by Goldilocks when it is the three bears who suffer the trauma of coming back to find that their home has been invaded, that they have been robbed, and that the interloper is asleep in one of their beds?

Bruce Beattie, London EC1.

☐ BEAR society is male dominated . . . the intended time of consumption was when Daddy Bear's porridge was just right, at which time Baby Bear's would have been too cold and Mummy Bear's would have congealed. It's just that Goldilocks got there early.

John Higgs, Stoneygate, Leicester.

☐ THE QUESTIONER assumes that Mummy Bear had the middle-sized portion. The fact that her porridge was cooler than her child's suggests that this was not so. There are two

probable reasons for Mummy Bear's small serving; both reflect badly on the state of equality in ursine society. Times were hard in the woods of fairytale land and porridge was often a rare commodity. If stocks were running low, it is all too likely that noble Mummy Bear would go without in order to fill the stomachs of her husband and child. Or, after pressure from the media and her partner, Mummy Bear may have become depressed about her ample figure (7ft tall, 22½ stone) and felt obliged to go on a diet.
M. Hewett, Connahs Quay, Clwyd.

□ NURSERY tales, like nursery rhymes, are hotbeds of cultural propaganda. Daddy Bear is a macho male — red-hot porridge, rock-hard bed. (You even see him on television, drinking beer with the lads.) Mummy Bear is a wimp. Baby Bear, with whom readers are intended to identify, is superior to Mummy, doing its level best to emulate Daddy, and the little brat is *always* right.
(Prof) Ian Stewart, Mathematics Institute, University of Warwick, Coventry.

QUESTION: Why do some tunes, like 'Nimrod' from Elgar's *Enigma Variations*, make you want to cry?

□ SOME music arouses sad or happy emotions because of past events that we associate with it (the 'Listen, darling, they're playing our tune' syndrome) but this doesn't account for the fact that some tunes seem to have the power to affect different individuals' emotions in an apparently similar way, even when the people concerned have no shared history of experience to account for this reaction. Music scholars and philosophers have long disputed whether or not music actually 'means' anything, and if so, what. The late Deryck Cooke comes closest, in my view, to explaining this contentious area of musical aesthetics. In his book, *The Language of Music* (OUP, 1959), Cooke suggests that all composers of tonal music from the Middle Ages to the mid-20th century have used the same 'language' of melodic phrases, harmonies and rhythms to evoke the same emotions in the listener. If true, this could account for the fact that 'Nimrod' seems to communicate the same feeling of melancholy to different people. This is a hideous oversimplification of Cooke's complex theory. He argues that it should be possible to compile a dictionary of musical idioms and their corresponding 'meanings' to identify which sequences of notes convey joy, grief, innocence, erotic love, etc.

Linda Barlow, Reading, Berks.

□ IT IS a very rare tune which would cause a listener to want to cry. But a harmonised piece of music can very easily do so. Music often depends for its interest on creating and resolving tension. Tension is given to a passage by, for instance, moving away from the key in which the piece started. When the 'home' key is returned to it comes with a feeling of resolution. The classical sonata form is basically an exercise in waiting for the return of the tonic key. Composers started to use devices such as a long dominant pedal (signalling that we are about to return to the home key) and then delaying the final resolution longer than expected, giving added weight to the home key when it is finally reached. Another way of creating and resolving tension is through dissonance. Two or more notes that do not sound pleasant together are changed for some that do. The more dissonant the interval, the more it can make you physically tense up (I find my neck and shoulders tightening). And probably the simplest trick of all is like a rhetorical device much loved by Hitler – start quietly and get louder. If you're really out to milk the emotions you are more subtle and reach the loudest point about nine-tenths of the way through and subside back to peacefulness. 'Nimrod' uses all of these tricks. The theme itself is harmonised using dissonances (some of which resolve into further dissonance, heightening the effect); it starts quietly and gradually builds up; just before the final statement of the theme there is a long roll on a timp while the brass extend the feeling of 'here we go back to the tonic key' by waffling in the dominant, and after the loudest bit of all it recedes to a quiet conclusion. Music can also make you cry if it is crap.

P. S. Lucas, Birmingham 18.

QUESTION: Whatever happened to nylon shirts?

☐ I SUSPECT they were withdrawn from the market because they don't wear out. I regularly use nylon shirts bought in the late 1960s and early 1970s. My wife adds that she still wears a Bri-Nylon cardigan acquired about 1950.

J. M. Lee, York.

☐ NYLON SHIRTS had a reputation for being uncomfortable in warm conditions — they would stick to the body, static would build up, and dirt gathered rapidly around the collar; these phenomena being due to the hydrophobic or non-water absorbing properties of the Nylon fibre. Despite these drawbacks they were tough, and hard wearing. That is until the late 1960s, when textile scientists blended Polyester and cotton fibres, usually in the ratios of 67:33 or 50:50 respectively, and found that a cloth could be produced which had all the advantages of a synthetic — low shrinkage, hardwearing and good crease recovery, along with the comfort and absorbency of cotton. Nylon/cotton blends were not considered a viable proposition due to difficulties in processing, one of which was the heat-setting of the nylon, which had to be carried out at a much higher temperature than the polyester. Shirts produced with the new polyester/cotton blends became very popular very quickly due to their hard-wearing nature, washability, shape retention, and most of all comfort. Nylon shirts were shunted off the market stall by

the increasingly cheaper polyester/cotton shirts and can now be found in jumble sales and washing buckets.
Peter Finan, Bradford, W. Yorks.

QUESTION: Is it true that goldfish have a memory span of only five seconds?

☐ WHEN STUDYING for the Biological Bases of Behaviour course of an Open University degree, one experiment I did was to investigate colour vision and learning ability in goldfish. Using three feeding tubes, one red, one green, one yellow, and otherwise identical, I established that my little goldfish quickly learned to distinguish which colour tube would release food, irrespective of position. It could distinguish each of the three colours and retained the knowledge overnight. When the fish had learnt to choose by colour, I altered the experiment so that position determined which tube would release food while the colour kept changing. The fish quickly learned to select the left-hand tube, then the right-hand tube, irrespective of colour. It even managed to return to selecting the left-hand tube, retaining the new knowledge overnight. Only during the very last change mentioned did it start to exhibit what I can only describe as signs of doubting and loss of self-confidence. When, finally I attempted to return to the original criteria of selection on the basis of colour, the poor fish showed all the signs of a full-blown breakdown. It hedged itself up in a corner of the tank, behind the water-weeds, not venturing out to feed even when food was freely available. It exhibited the signs of self-doubt and an inability to cope with life. I felt dreadful about this, my betrayal of its trust, as it seemed to me. I stopped the experiment and the fish was retired to the comfort and companionship of a friend's pond. There is little doubt that this goldfish could 'remember' for longer than five seconds.

(Mrs) P. A. Bailey, Stourbridge, W Midlands.

□ FOR a fish with a good memory try a piranha. They have a megabyte.
Philip King, Camberwell, London.

QUESTION: In mythology and elsewhere, one encounters references to fearsome maelstroms, giant marine whirlpools in fixed locations. Do any exist today?

□ THE GARAFALO, off northern Sicily, is thought to be the mythical Charybdis mentioned in Homer's *Odyssey*. Whirlpools are caused by the clash of two tides, coupled with the uneven ocean floor. When two tides fail to coincide and synchronise, large circular eddies can result. But Garafalo is not a true whirlpool since it forms no vortices. A good example of a whirlpool is the Corryvrekan off the coast of Craobh Haven, between the Hebridean islands of Jura and Scorba. In 1951 it claimed the motor cruiser, Dewey Red, after the four-man crew abandoned her following technical problems; all that was left was a small amount of flotsam. The British Admiralty says of the Corryvrekan in its publi-

cation, *The West Coast of Scotland Pilot:* 'Navigation is at times most hazardous and no stranger under any circumstances can be justified in attempting it.' Other good examples of this phenomenon can be found off St Malo, Brittany, north-west France, and the Naruto Strait off the Japanese city of Osaka. These aquatic wonders do occasionally cause shipping some problems, but most, if not all, are well-documented, and their ferocity and vehemence has been overstated to a large degree, in both legend and in literature.
Mike Hurley, Doncaster, S. Yorkshire.

☐ IN 1947, George Orwell's life almost ended when he took some friends with him in his boat through the Corryvrekan. He miscalculated the tide and the boat was caught in a whirlpool, the engine fell off, and the boat turned upside down. They were stranded on a small island until some lobster fishermen rescued them. The whirlpool is situated in Scotland between the isle of Jura north coast and the isle of Scarba. I believe the Royal Navy consider the Gulf to be unnavigable.
S. M. Mamling, Ashford, Kent.

☐ AT SALTSTRAUMEN, in Norway, a conflux of currents caused by the topography of the fjords creates a whirlpool, which apparently is at its most violent at high tide when the moon is full or new. This is probably the maelstrom referred to in Edgar Allan Poe's story, 'A Descent into the Maelstrom', though Poe exaggerated its power. Details of how to get to Saltstraumen are in *The Rough Guide To Scandinavia*.
Andrew Spencer, New Malden, Surrey.

☐ ALTHOUGH I am grateful to Andrew Spencer for pointing out that my *Rough Guide To Scandinavia* does indeed give details of how to get to the natural maelstrom at Saltstraumen in Norway, I fear he is mistaken when he identifies this as the maelstrom referred to in Poe's story. As my book

points out a couple of pages further on, Poe's maelstrom is in fact the one known as the Moskenstraumen, at a place called A in the Norwegian Lofoten Islands. Dedicated whirlpool watchers could do worse than to snap up my Rough Guide To Sicily, too, which features details of the mythical Charybdis. As there aren't any whirlpools in Hong Kong, it would be shameless self-publicity to mention that I've just written a book about there as well.
Jules Brown, Rough Guides, London SE11.

QUESTION: If two perfect spheres come into contact, how can the area of touch be calculated?

☐ THE AREA of contact can be calculated quite easily. In fact two perfect spheres can only be in contact with each other over that puzzling, yet exact, mathematical region, known as the 'point'. This means that whatever the sizes of the spheres in question, the area of touch between them is always zero. This fact is of great comfort to all bad snooker players, since the probability of striking a non-existing area of one snooker ball against a non-existing area of another is negligible, if not in fact zero. Professional players have got round this problem, however, by suggesting that the elastic properties of even the hardest snooker balls, together with the impossibility of manufacturing a mathematically perfect spherical ball, allows for a finite area of contact between balls on impact. I reject this hypothesis, however, and will continue to boycott a sport which I consider to be a mathematical impossibility.
Steve Williamson, Liverpool 15.

☐ WHEN the two spheres first meet they touch at a single point. Under the slightest load, the spheres elastically deform to give a very small circular contact patch. Using the theory of elastic contact worked out by Heinrich Hertz at the age of 24 in 1882, the area A of this patch is given by the formula below (the subscripts refer to the spheres, P is the load, v is Poisson's ratio, E is the elastic modulus, and R is the sphere radius). The assumptions made in this analysis should apply for the 'perfect' spheres in question. See any book on contact mechanics for details.

James Cole, Research Assistant, Tribology Section, Mechanical Engineering, Imperial College, London SW7.

$$A = \pi \left\{ \frac{3P}{4} \left[\frac{1-v_1^2}{E_1} + \frac{1-v_2^2}{E_2} \right] \left(\frac{R_1 R_2}{R_1+R_2} \right) \right\}^{\frac{2}{3}}$$

QUESTION: Quite often I have my cotton socks 'blessed'. Can anyone tell me the origin of this saying?

☐ GEORGE Edward Lynch Cotton became Bishop of Calcutta in 1858 and while there established schools for Eurasian children. A man of great sensitivity, he ordered crates full of socks for the children, to be worn during lessons. It was the rule of the Bishop to bless all goods which arrived at the schools. A zealous member of staff one day distributed socks before the blessing, so thereafter every time a shipment arrived a note was placed on them to the effect: 'Cotton's socks for blessing'. Cotton's socks soon became corrupted to cotton socks. When the Bishop was drowned in the Ganges on October 6, 1866, a despatch was sent to the Archbishop to ask: 'Who will bless his cotton socks?'
(Mrs) Jane M. Glossop, Pwllheli, Gwynedd.

QUESTION: Recipes including red kidney beans always say the beans must be soaked and boiled, and the cooking water discarded before use. What is the

toxin in red beans, and is it destroyed by heat or dissolved in the water?

☐ RED KIDNEY beans contain compounds called lectins (haemagglutinins) which form part of the plant's natural defensive systems, offering protection against insect and herbivore predators. Lectins are wholly, or partly, protein in structure and thus their biological effects are destroyed by moist heat. The beans should be thoroughly soaked to allow the water to fully penetrate, and swell, the tissue. Boiling is essential because at lower temperatures not all of the lectin will be inactivated and some toxicity will remain. When it was fashionable partially to cook red kidney beans, for example, for use in salads, many cases of gastrointestinal disturbance and 'food poisoning' were reported. While little of the lectin will be removed by soaking alone, this process may remove very much smaller compounds such as saponins (which give the washing water its 'soapy' feel) and oligosaccharides – which are a cause of intestinal gas and social discomfort. Lectins are found in many different legumes, the seeds generally being the richest source. Red, white, brown, and black kidney beans, runner beans and tepary beans are among the most toxic in the raw state. All lectins have an affinity for sugars, such as occur in the membranes of cells. When lectins bind to sugars in the cells of the intestinal wall they interfere with nutrient absorption and cause reduced growth, diarrhoea, intestinal discomfort and increased incidence of bacterial infection.
G. R. Fenwick, Institute for Food Research, Norwich.

QUESTION: When, where and how were larks' tongues eaten?

☐ THE SUBJECT is mentioned in the historical novel, *Claudius the God*, by Robert Graves, in the section dealing with the life of Herod Agrippa: 'Herod invited Caligula to the

most expensive banquet that had ever been given in the city [Rome]; unheard-of delicacies were served, including five great pastries entirely filled with the tongues of tit-larks, marvellously delicate fish brought in tanks all the way from India, and for the roast an animal like a young elephant, but hairy and of no known species – it had been found embedded in the ice of some frozen lake of the Caucasus.'
Oliver Stephenson, Faversham, Kent.

☐ IF THEY were eaten anywhere it would indeed be ancient Rome or any great city of the empire. Robert Graves may have invented the pie of tit-lark tongues, but perhaps he found a reference in the famous Roman cookbook of Apicius (1st century AD), whose recipe for flamingo tongue ragout was enjoyed by Caligula. Or the detail may have come from Pliny, who in his *Natural History* said he was disgusted that Apicius had taught that flamingo tongues were delicious (10.68). They were much enjoyed by gourmands, Martial comments in an epigram (13.71), but he too looked askance on the taste. The emperor Elagabalus (AD 218–222) was supposed often to have eaten nightingales' tongues. The Romans were fond of eating tiny birds called fig-peckers, which Graves may have rendered as tit-larks. I always thought the ultimate delicacy was larks' tongues in aspic.
Ilona Jesnick, London N14.

QUESTION: Why 'Piggy Bank'? Why not lamb, cow or donkey bank?

☐ THIS originates from about the 16th century. The pig is the only farm animal that is of value only when dead. Thus the 'bank', traditionally made out of china, was so designed that it had to be broken in order to be opened – symbolically 'killing the pig'. Other farm animals do not have to be killed

before they are of use. For instance, the cow can be milked, the bull put to stud, eggs obtained from hens and so on.
R. Thomas, Bridgend, Mid-Glamorgan.

☐ IT APPEARS that livestock farming is not R. Thomas's forte. Sows and boars produce progeny, like cows and bulls, ewes and rams. Like fattening pigs, fattening cattle and fattening lambs are also 'of value only when dead', to use Mr Thomas's unfortunate phrase, which is also, however, a far from accurate statement. Perhaps the answer is simpler: because it was only this little piggy that went to market?
John Nix, Emeritus Professor of Farm Business Management, Wye College, Ashford, Kent.

☐ AT ONE time, people used to keep their money in pots made of a type of earthenware called pigge. These so-called 'pigge banks', were not at first made in the shape of pigs, but presumably some manufacturer thought it was funny to do so.
Peter Morris, Norwich.

☐ THE PIG is an ancient symbol of wordly wealth throughout China and Southeast Asia. Pottery models of pigs were made as funerary offerings and were often stuffed with paper 'money' specially made for funerary purposes. The earliest example of a piggy-bank I have seen is a 12th–13th century Majapahit terracotta of a very chubby pig from Java. It is hollow with a thin slot in the top of its back. Similar piggy-banks were produced in Java and Sumatra between the 12th and 17th centuries. Since the earliest European example I have seen is an early Delft blue and white piggy bank dating from around 1610, I have always assumed that the Dutch imported the design from Indonesia.
Nigel Palmer, London SW15.

QUESTION: Why are crossword puzzles set out symmetrically?

□ THE MODERN crossword evolved from a puzzle by Arthur Wynne, a Liverpool immigrant, in *The New York Sunday World*, December 21, 1913, described as a Word-Cross. Although Wynne thought it 'just another puzzle' it attracted great enthusiasm from the readers, becoming a regular feature immediately. The basic rules were formulated from suggestions from readers refined to popular taste. A symmetrical grid became a convention within months. There is a certain pleasing elegance about the cryptic 'half-light' symmetrical grid (where about half the letters in a word are shared with other words). Most newspapers have a number of sets, usually about 30 grids, available to their compilers who choose which one to use. Some syndicated puzzles in evening papers have 12 grids used in sequence so that alternate Mondays, say, will use the same grid. All these grids are symmetrical.
Roger F. Squires (listed in the Guinness Book of Records *as The World's Most Prolific Crossword Compiler'), Telford, Shropshire.*

□ BESIDES the 'pleasing elegance' of a symmetrical grid, there are distinct advantages from the point of view of checking and proof-reading. The position of the black squares can be quickly checked by folding the grid in half and holding it up to the light. Furthermore, the solution lengths given in brackets after the Across clues also follow a pattern of symmetry. If one starts with the first Across clue and reads the solution lengths down to the middle Across clue, a sequence is found which is repeated by starting with the final Across clue and reading upwards to the middle again. Thus, the symmetrical grid is preferred by puzzle checkers employing these methods, as we do in our offices every day.
Rick Hosburn, Puzzles Editor, Take a Break, *London NW1.*

☐ RICK HOSBURN suggests that a symmetrical crossword is easier to check, since the position of the black squares can be checked by folding the crossword and holding it up to the light. I've tried this on today's Quick Crossword in the *Guardian* and it doesn't work, since the symmetry is in a diagonal plane. The argument that the length of clues is easier to check is also a false one. All Mr Hosburn proves is that it is easy to check that a symmetrical crossword is in fact symmetrical − hardly a valid reason for using symmetrical crosswords in the first place. I postulate that the real reason for crosswords being symmetrical is simply 'because they are'.
Tim Cresswell, Leeds.

☐ WHEN we used to compile crosswords we were helped by the basic rule that you fill in black squares alternately on alternate rows. Since you can put your first black in any one of the four squares in the top left hand corner this gives four immediate variations. If you now fill in more blacks symmetrically and tidily you avoid impossible tangles of letters and/or a plethora of two-letter words. Any less disciplined approach leads to insanity. How do the people who make 'all-white' crosswords manage?
John & Hazel Sweetman, Basingstoke.

QUESTION: What is the origin of the crescent moon symbol seen throughout Islamic cultures?

☐ ISLAM emerged in Arabia where travel along the desert trade routes was largely by night, and navigation depended upon the position of the moon and stars. The moon thus represents the guidance of God on the path through life. The new moon also represents the Muslim calendar, which has 12 months each of 29 or 30 days. So in Islam the lunar month and the calendar month coincide, and the new moon is eagerly awaited, especially at the end of the month of

Ramadan when its sighting means that the celebrations of 'Id al-Fitr can begin.
Linda and Phil Holmes, Cottingham, N. Humberside.

☐ THE USE of the so-called crescent moon in many Islamic symbols cannot be related to the importance attached to the new moon in Islam. The moon depicted on e.g. many Islamic flags is the old moon, the reverse shape of the new moon, which is like a letter C backwards. Again 'crescent', implying 'increasing', is properly applicable only to the young moon: the old moon is diminishing in phase. Presumably the moon is depicted as a crescent in Islamic, and many other, contexts as that shape is unambiguously lunar.
A. A. Davis, London SW7.

☐ ALTHOUGH the crescent is indeed a very widespread motif in Islamic iconography, it is not Islamic in origin nor exclusive to that religion. The emblem has been used in Christian art for many centuries in depictions of the Virgin Mary, for example. It is in fact one of the oldest icons in human history, having been known in graphic depictions since at least as early as the Babylonian period in Mesopotamia. The stele of Ur Namu, for example, dating from 2100 BC, includes the crescent moon to symbolise the god Sin, along with a star representing Shamash, the sun god. Later the moon became a female deity, typified by the goddess Artemis and her many counterparts, including Diana, who was celebrated as the moon-goddess in Roman times and depicted with a crescent on her brow. The device seems to have entered Islam via the Seljuk Turks who dominated Anatolia in the 12th century, and was widely used by their successors, the Ottoman Turks, who eventually became the principal Islamic nation, and whose Sultan held the title of Caliph until 1922. The story that the Ottomans adopted the crescent to symbolise their conquest of Constantinople must be dismissed as mere legend, since the device considerably predates 1453. In the late 19th century the Pan-Islamic movement, sponsored by the Sultan Abdul Hamid II, used the crescent and star on a green flag as part of its propaganda, and from this were derived the flags of Egypt and Pakistan and many other Islamic states.

William G. Crampton, Director of the Flag Institute, Chester.

☐ A DETAILED answer will be found in the entry 'Hilal' *Encyclopaedia of Islam* (second edition, Brill, Leiden, 1960). Professor Richard Ettinghausen, writer of the entry, notes that crescent moon (hilal) motif is featured with a five or six pointed star (the latter known as Solomon's shield in the Islamic world) on early Islamic coins circa AD 695, but it carried no distinct Islamic connotation. Some 500 years later, it appears in association with various astrological/ astronomical symbols on 12th-century Islamic metal-work, but when depicted in manuscript painting, held by a seated man, it is thought to represent the authority of a high court official: 'the sun [is] to the king and the moon [is] to the vizier'. Its use as a roof finial on Islamic buildings also dates from this medieval period but the motif still had no specific religious meaning, as it decorated all types of architecture, secular as well as religious. In fact Ettinghausen argues that it was the European assumption that this was a religious and national emblem that led to several Muslim governments adopting it officially during the 19th century.

(Dr) Patricia Baker, Farnham, Surrey.

QUESTION: When sugar rationing ended in 1953, was this followed by an increase in tooth decay?

☐ YES, indeed, there was a marked increase. This was found, for example, by Professor Peter James of Birmingham University among British children. Conversely, when sugar consumption dropped during wartime, decay rates also dropped, not only in Britain but elsewhere in Europe. Professor Sogannaes (from Norway) reviewed 27 wartime studies covering 750,000 children in 11 European countries and found that the decay rate was reduced on average by over 50 per cent. When sugar rationing stopped, the decay rates returned to pre-war levels within a few years. Sugar consumption in Britain has remained high since the 1950s. That is why so many people still suffer from tooth decay, despite some protection from fluoridated toothpastes. It is worth stressing that sugar is the sole cause of tooth decay. This is a scientifically well-established relationship although the pro-sugar lobby tries to cast doubt on it.

(Prof.) Aubrey Sheiham, Dept of Community Dental Health, University College, London.

QUESTION: Is the bleeping at the beginning of the *Inspector Morse* theme tune Morse Code, and if so what is the message?

☐ HOW pleasing to report that the Morse Code in the theme to *Inspector Morse* actually spells the word 'Morse'. There are all too few examples of well-sent Morse in contemporary drama, although unintended Morse messages are quite common. A friend of mine swears that the phrasing of the theme to *Some Mothers Do 'Ave 'Em* is pretty disgusting although I've never heard it that way myself. You can, if you wish, sing the opening bars of the US National Anthem to 'dot-dot-dash-dot dot-dot-dash dash-dot-dash-dot dash-dot-dash', which I think you will agree, is really pretty tasteless; and as for that thrush in my back garden . . .

Roger Williams, Ashridge Management College, Berkhamstead, Herts.

☐ UNFORTUNATELY it spells 'TTORSE', the composer having spread out the dashes of the 'M'. In my days as an amateur radio transmitter in the 1930s, the composer would have been accused of having a glass arm.

W. J. Crawley, Torquay.

QUESTION: In chapter five of *English History 1914–45***, A. J. P. Taylor states: 'The passport was, of course, required by foreign governments. British citizens do not need a passport to leave this country in peacetime or to return to it.' Is this still the case?**

☐ YES, A. J. P. Taylor was right, one can leave the UK and return without a passport – although strictly speaking this does not apply if one is flying. Clause 42 of Magna Carta states: 'Any freeman may travel abroad without let or hindrance of the King and return safe and secure by land and by water except in the time of war.' I know because several years ago our son found his passport was out of date late in the day before he was due to go on holiday with his girlfriend. The Public Records Office looked it up for me and explained that France, his destination, could refuse to let him in, but in July at the height of the holiday season the French authorities probably would not notice his passport was out of date. I was advised, however, that he should have on him the above Magna Carta clause, in case his exit from or re-entry to this country was queried with an out-of-date passport.
(Mrs) V. M. Crews, Beckenham, Kent.

☐ BRITISH citizens aren't citizens as such but only subjects of the Crown and we do need the permission of the Sovereign to leave the country – otherwise we might all leave to avoid unpleasant wars and taxes and the like. Rather than take up her time writing letters allowing her trusty and well-beloved Waynes and Traceys to spend their fortnights in Ibiza, the Queen provides these passport substitutes. If you don't want to carry one, you could petition the Queen for a leave-giving letter, which might make quite an impressive travel document.
Humphrey Evans, London, N7.

☐ DEPARTURE from the UK, with some important exceptions is not subject to control but entry is. Taylor's remark is technically truer now than it was then because at that time 'British Citizen' was a phrase which had no legal definition. British subjects, including Commonwealth citizens, had the right freely to enter and remain in the UK before the nationality legislation of the 1960s which sought to control certain categories of 'coloured' immigration. The phrase 'British Citizen' was adopted in 1981 to define those who have the right of abode in the UK and do not require leave to enter. With the exception of a number of Citizens of the UK and Colonies under the previous nationality acts, others require leave and can be refused entry or have conditions placed on their stay. This includes many people who have only one of the limited forms of British nationality and Commonwealth citizens who are still British subjects. For immigration purposes a passport is evidence of identity, nationality (or citizenship) and (in the case of the UK) the person's immigration status. It is these factors, not the passport itself, which determine a person's entitlement to enter the UK. So the possession of a passport is not essential. The right to enter without leave is dependent on a legal status: having the right of abode. Principle aside, it's important for all and essential for many with the right of abode to have a passport. Anyone arriving without a passport has to convince the immigration officer at the port of entry that she has the right of abode and if she is unsuccessful may be refused entry. Until recently, such a person was entitled to remain in the UK for the purpose of an appeal. Under the Immigration Act 1988, however, a person arriving without a passport which shows right of abode (as British Citizen or otherwise) can't remain in the UK while waiting for the appeal to be heard, and needs leave to come to the UK to be at the appeal. But the non-passport holder may never get to that point. Under the Immigration (Carriers' Liability) Act 1987, carriers by sea or air are liable to pay on demand £1,000 for every passenger requiring leave who fails to

produce a valid passport or other document establishing identity and nationality or citizenship, and a visa if applicable. Although this does not apply to those with the right of abode, the carrier may be unable to establish or unwilling to assume that a person without a passport has the right of abode. If so, you won't get on the boat or the plane.
C. R. Bradley, School of Law, Polytechnic of Central London.

☐ IN 1973 I travelled from Heathrow to the Netherlands without a passport. I had quite a job to persuade the UK emigration officer to let me out of the country but he let me go reluctantly after I asked him if he could quote an act of parliament requiring British citizens to have a passport (I was sure that there wasn't one). The Dutch appropriate official, a member of the police force, when told I had no passport merely smiled and said welcome to the Netherlands.
Herbert Layton, Gloucester.

☐ SOME years ago a French immigration officer, after studying for a few moments the passport my husband had handed him, remarked quite politely that it was difficult to believe he was only 10 years old. My pre-occupied spouse had mistakenly taken not his own but our younger son's passport with him on this solo journey; embarrassed and dismayed, he began apologising and explaining, but had hardly begun before the officer stamped the passport and handed it back to him with a shrug – a Gallic shrug, no doubt.
Merivan Coles, London SW5.

QUESTION: What is the difference, if any, between cups of tea prepared by putting in the tea or the milk first?

☐ I WAS told by a former resident of Imperial India that, if the quality of the milk was in doubt, then putting the milk in

first was a more effective way of scalding it and killing the bacteria. Thus it would seem that to ask for 'milk in first' when taking tea with the Duchess is a subtle way of criticising her standard of housekeeping.
Vic Smith, Uxbridge, Middx.

□ THE PRACTICE of putting the milk in first originated when users of fine china decided it was hazardous to pour in the hot tea first, in case the cups broke. Thereafter it was a matter of snobbery.
(Mrs) M. Ringrose, London SW18.

□ IN THE teacup, two chemical reactions take place which alter the protein of the milk: denaturing and tanning. The first, the change that takes place in milk when it is heated, depends only on temperature. 'Milk-first' gradually brings the contents of the cup up from fridge-cool. 'Milk-last' rapidly heats the first drop of milk almost to the temperature of the teapot, denaturing it to a greater degree and so developing more 'boiled milk' flavour. The second reaction is analogous to the tanning of leather. Just as the protein of untanned hide is combined with tannin to form chemically tough collagen/tannin complexes, so in the teacup, the milk's protein turns into tannin/casein complexes. But there is a difference: in leather every reactive point on the protein molecule is taken up by a tannin molecule, but this need not be so in tea. Unless the brew is strong enough to tan all the casein completely, 'milk-first' will react differently from 'milk-last' in the way it distributes the tannin through the casein. In 'milk-first', all the casein tans uniformly; in milk-last' the first molecules of casein entering the cup tan more thoroughly than the last ones. If the proportions of tannin to casein are near to chemical equality, 'which-first' may determine whether some of the casein escapes tanning entirely. There is no reason why this difference should not alter the taste.
Dan Lowy, Sutton, Surrey.

☐ FOR further enlightenment, we should turn to George Orwell and his essay, 'A Nice Cup Of Tea' (*Evening Standard*, 1946). 'The Milk First school can bring forward some fairly strong arguments,' he wrote, 'but I maintain that my own argument is unanswerable. This is that, by putting the tea in first and then stirring as one pours, one can exactly regulate the amount of milk, whereas one is liable to put in too much milk the other way round.'
David Beech, Cotham, Bristol.

MINISTRY OF SILLY WALKS.

QUESTION: When, where and by whom was the 'goose-step' style of marching introduced, and was there any logical reason for its use?

☐ LEOPOLD of Anhalt-Dessau, known as 'Old Snoutnose', set psalms to march tunes and devised the 54 movements of Prussian drill, including the ceremonial march-past with unbent leg that came to be known as the goose-step.
(Mrs) Grace Abbott, Gravesend, Kent.

QUESTION: What do BBC newsreaders type into their machines at the end of the news? Why is it necessary to do this?

☐ THEY are merely 'logging off' from the BASYS computer system terminal on the desk (as required by the Data Protection Act). Doing so while in vision is probably a little theatrical device like the famous non-functioning telephone for conducting live interviews. Perhaps more interesting is to ask why the terminal is on the desk anyway. The BASYS system can instantly show any information within it on the autocue, though this function is not normally used by the presenter. However, each terminal can be programmed to receive incoming 'flashes' which can be useful for late football scores, etc. That is how I use it during the regional bulletin each evening, but perhaps my colleagues in London are more advanced users . . .
Phil Sayer, news presenter, BBC North, Manchester.

☐ THE PRESENT fad for closing bulletins with a prolonged shot leaves the newscaster in an activity void which is filled by pretending to have a conversation with the co-presenter or fiddling with bits of paper. Button-pushing, I suspect, is the latest assimilated activity meant to impress us with a little touch of high tech.
J. Williamson, Sevenoaks, Kent.

QUESTION: Has any attempt ever been made to salvage King John's treasure from The Wash?

☐ FOR some 60 years a body called the Wash Research Committee sought the treasure. In 1956 Dr George Tagg, of the Chiswick firm Evershed & Vignoles Ltd, started probing reclaimed land near Sutton Bridge, looking for the causeway where King John's baggage train was said to have been overcome by the tide in 1216. In 1961 a group from the

Central Council for Physical Recreation were set to bore holes for Dr Tagg. It was believed that the Wash Research Committee and Dr Tagg had located a causeway across the estuary of the old Wellstream. In 1963 Nottingham University volunteers believed they had found something hard after boring 25 feet below reclaimed farmland near Wisbech. Analysis, it was said, disclosed traces of gold, silver and copper. A full-scale investigation today would cost a fortune. Dr Tagg failed to come up with any treasure. He believed it was buried up to 60 feet below the soil.
Leslie Jerman, Theydon Bois, Essex.

QUESTION: What happened to the Noise Abatement Society, so influential in the 1960s?

☐ THE SOCIETY was so successful that nothing has been heard of it since the 1970s.
Robin Boyes, Burniston, Scarborough, Yorks.

☐ THE SOCIETY is alive and well and is stepping up its environmental education campaign to reduce noise from neighbours. We are deluged with pitiful appeals from victims, who are driven to desperation by noise which they are unable to stop or escape. Frustration, loss of sleep and fear of violence from the noisemakers if they complain to the authorities seriously affects their mental and physical health and reduces their efficiency. We give them information, advice and practical help. Legislation does exist, with maximum penalties of a £2,000 fine and six months imprisonment, but it is very difficult to enforce and the costs of doing so are horrendous. So we feel that the only real and lasting solution lies in persuasion and education of the public to show respect for people's rights to peace and quiet. We are happy to respond to inquiries, which should be addressed to PO Box No. 8, Bromley, Kent, BR2 0UH, enclosing a stamped, self-addressed envelope. Education and persua-

sion are expensive operations and we have just launched a charitable appeal to help pay for them.
John Connell, Noise Abatement Society.

QUESTION: Are scientists any closer to answering the question: which came first, the chicken or the egg?

☐ ASSUMING that the chicken evolved from two other birds which were not quite chickens, then these two latter birds must have produced, at some time in the past, an egg out of which came the first chicken.
Geoffrey Samuel, Lancaster.

☐ WE MUST remember that the chicken is an *actual* chicken whereas the egg is only a *potential* chicken. Philosophically speaking, actuality always precedes potentiality, so the chicken came first. Probably.
Kishor Alam, London N14.

☐ KISHOR Alam argues on the basis of actuality preceding potentiality that the chicken must come before the egg. But from the egg's point of view, a chicken is only a potential egg (just as human beings are simply the way genes manage to perpetuate themselves).
David Lewis, St Albans, Herts.

☐ THE CHICKEN is, of course, *Archaeopteryx*, the oldest fossil bird. It comes from the Solnhofen Lithograhic Limestone, from the late Jurassic rocks of Bavaria (that is about 150 million years ago). Its skeleton is so like that of contemporary dinosaurs that it is generally agreed that its ancestors were in fact small, lightly built dinosaurs. The dinosaurs were reptiles, and in some cases are known to have laid eggs, therefore it is likely that the egg came first. However, most fossil reptile eggs date from the later Cretaceous period (144 to 65 million years ago) and are those of large dinosaurs –

large and relatively strong eggs which have a better chance
of preservation than smaller ones. The oldest find reported
(from the Early Permian – about 270 million years ago – of
Texas) is so poorly preserved that palaeontologists are
uncertain about its true identity. It may be the remains of an
inorganic nodule – a chemical growth within the sediment.
The earliest reptile fossils come from even older rocks: the
Early Carboniferous (350 million years ago) of Scotland. So
it is probable that the earliest eggs date from this time – 200
million years before *Archaeopteryx*. The egg is no chicken!
*(Dr) Denis Bates, Institute of Earth Studies, University
College of Wales, Aberystwyth.*

☐ READERS may be interested in the rather tongue-in-cheek
article by Walter N. Thurman and Mark E. Fisher: 'Chicken,
Eggs, and Causality, or Which Came First?' (*American
Journal of Agricultural Economics*, May 1988). The authors
conducted so-called 'Granger causality tests' using annual
data from the US Department of Agriculture on egg production and chicken population covering the period 1930–83.
Such tests can be used to see if there is an asymmetry
between the value of the information provided by past
observations of the variables in predicting each other's
current values. Using regression analysis one attempts to
discover whether variations in a series Y (say chicken population) can be adequately, explained by its own past values,
or whether lagged values of a second variable X (say egg
production) contribute significantly to the equation. A similar regression would be carried out reversing the role of the
variables. If it can be shown that X is needed to help explain
Y (after accounting for the influence of past values of Y) but
that Y is not needed to explain movements in X, then one
may conclude that X 'Granger-causes' Y (after Clive
Granger who first proposed the procedure). Using this
approach in what Thurman and Fisher called 'the most
natural application of tests for Granger causality' they
concluded that the egg came first. However, readers may feel

that this result should be taken with a pinch of salt, especially when they hear that other applications of the test have given rise to such perverse findings as 'GNP "causes" sunspot activity!'
Guy Judge, Emsworth, Hants.

QUESTION: **Some years ago I read about an Irish monk, living in the 10th century, who predicted the number of popes who would succeed to office before the divine judgment. For each pope he gave a short description, some of which have proved apposite. What was the name of the monk? How is the present pope described?**

☐ ST MALACHY of Ireland (1095–1148) was renowned for his prophecies during his lifetime; however, the series of two- and three-word descriptions of popes from 1143 to the end of the papacy – 111 in all – which was published in his name in 1595 is now generally accepted to be a forgery. The descriptions are usually rather vague, and require a certain amount of creative interpretation on the part of the reader: for instance, the prophecy relating to John XXIII, *Pastor et*

nauta, is held to refer to that pope's role as 'shepherd and navigator' of the Second Vatican Council. The current pope, John Paul II, is described as *De labore solis*, 'from the labour of the sun', a typically opaque phrase capable of any number of interpretations. There are only two popes remaining after John Paul II: they are signified *De gloria olivae* ('the glory of the olives') and *Petrus Romanus* ('Peter of Rome'). During the reign of the last-named pontiff, Rome will be destroyed and the Day of Judgment will come to pass.
Steve Duffy, Betws-yn-Rhos, Clwyd.

QUESTION: What is Plasticine? When and by whom was it invented?

☐ IT WAS invented in 1897 by my great great grandfather, William Harbutt (1844–1921) when he was an art teacher in Bath. It was a substitute for the clay used by his students which tended to dry out between lessons and was also messy. First mixings of Plasticine were carried out in the basement of his home in Bath using buckets and a garden roller to roll it out flat. The ingredients are a secret but are basically a fine powder mixed with various 'liquid' greases with colouring and perfume added. With the success of his modelling material, William bought an old flour mill at Bathampton, near Bath, and on May Day, 1900, full scale commercial production was started. The firm remained on the site under the name 'Harbutt's Plasticine' until the 1980s. It passed out of the control of the Harbutt family in 1976.
Tessa Harbutt, Marlow, Bucks.

☐ PLASTICINE is a blend of calcium salts, long chain aliphatic acids and petroleum jelly filled with whiting and suitably pigmented to produce a range of vibrant colours. Plasticine, which is a registered trademark, is now made by us to its original formula.
David Dooley, Peter Pan Playthings, Bretton, Peterborough.

QUESTION: Many years ago I saw D. W. Griffith's film, *Intolerance.* **In one scene, depicting the fall of Babylon in 586 BC, an actor's head appears to be cut off and rolls across the floor. The audience were told that a real actor had had his head removed by accident. Can this be true?**

☐ JOSEPH HENABURY, assistant director and actor in *Intolerance,* was 'surprised by the sadism' of the extras in the Babylonian sequence. He has been quoted as saying: 'We put part of the mobs up on the walls of Babylon. The Persian army would flood across the ground below, attacking, shooting their arrows and all that sort of thing. We gave the boys above bows and arrows, spears and what we called magnesium bombs, which were historically accurate. We'd take a roll of chicken wire, cover it with canvas, and coat it with magnesium. The men above would light their bombs and hurl them on the Persians below. How delighted they were when they could hit a guy who was supposed to be dead! When you saw a dead guy leap to his feet and run you knew someone was throwing bombs or plugging arrows at him' (quoted in Kevin Brownlow's book, *The Parade's Gone By*). But did such pranks extend to actual decapitation? Here is Brownlow again, this time in his book, *Hollywood, The Pioneers:* 'The violence was upsetting, too: I remember the shock of seeing the film for the first time when I was 13. Some mischievous friend had assured me that an extra was accidentally beheaded during the making of the film and, when I saw Elmo Lincoln lop the head off a Persian, I was so shaken I couldn't sleep for a week.' A definitive statement is given by Karl Brown, assistant cameraman on *Intolerance* in the book *Adventures With D. W. Griffith:* 'There was an awful lot of swordplay. In one scene an Assyrian's head was cut clean off by a single slash of a sword – dummy head, of course.' As I recall from a relatively recent TV showing of the film, the effect is achieved by jump-cutting from live actor to

dummy so quickly that it's hard to register the switch without the aid of a video freeze-frame.
Neil Hornick, London NW11.

QUESTION: During the 1960s there were notices scattered around the countryside which said three things: 1: Take nothing but photographs. 2: Leave nothing but footprints. What was the third piece of advice?

☐ KILL nothing but time.
Sheila Carter, Chelmsford, Essex.

QUESTION: How many Africans were transported to the Americas as a result of the European slave trade? Has anyone tried to quantify how many died as a result?

☐ ESTABLISHING a figure for the number of African slaves landed in the Americas between the 15th and 19th centuries is difficult, given the paucity of the statistics and also given that, after the early 19th century, such a trade was illegal for most Europeans and thus clandestine; any figures that are suggested inevitably are by way of estimates. In the 19th century a common estimate for the number of slaves landed in the Americas was to the order of 20 million or above. Some speak of double that. The debate on the totals was reopened by an American scholar, Philip Curtin, in his *The Atlantic Slave Trade: a Census* (1969), who came up with an estimated total of 9,566,100 slaves landed in the Americas (plus or minus approximately one million). This was revised upwards by J. E. Inikori in *The Journal of African History* vol 17, (1976) to around 15,400,000 slaves exported from Africa, and around 13,392,000 landed in the Americas. More recently, Paul Lovejoy in *Transformations in Slavery* (1983) has calculated a figure of 11,698,000 exported from Africa and around 9,900,000 landed. The debate is by no means closed and further work is liable to refine the totals more precisely. It must be remembered that this concerns the Atlantic slave trade; to these totals would have to be added figures for the numbers of slaves exported in the Indian Ocean trade to Arabia, and also the trans-Saharan trade into the Mediterranean world, in order to establish a figure for the overall demographic impact of the export of Africa's population during these centuries. For mortality in the Atlantic trade, figures vary widely, depending on the period concerned and the length of voyage and destination involved. Equally, even fewer statistics exist for this than for the numbers landed in the Americas. A common estimate often used by historians is of a mortality rate of approximately one-sixth of those exported from Africa.

(Dr) Martin Lynn, Dept of Modern History, The Queen's University of Belfast.

QUESTION: What is the exact fractional value of π – not 22/7, which is a commonly accepted approximation, but the fraction used to compute π to the millionth decimal place?

☐ THERE can't be any exact fraction for π: the mathematician, J H Lambert, proved this in the 1760s. What computers use to get to a large number of decimal places is one or another of several repetitive processes. These processes give closer approximations the longer they are carried on – without ever getting to an exactly correct value. For example, one process goes like this: start with 2 as the first term. Use this to start a subtotal. Multiply this first term by 1/3 to get the second term. Add the second term to the subtotal. Multiply the second term by 2/5 to make the third term. Add this to the subtotal. Carry on, always keeping the latest term to make the next, using as successive multipliers 3/7, 4/9, 5/11, 6/13, and so on. The subtotals gradually approach π.

Meanwhile, if 22/7 is too rough (error about one part in 2000), there is another fraction much closer to π, 355/113. This value was known in China around AD 470 and discovered in Europe about 1600. Its error is less than one part in ten million – surely close enough for most practical purposes!
Terry Stancliffe, London SW19.

☐ A MORE enjoyable way of calculating π is based on the Monte Carlo Method (it is essentially random). Draw a large square on a piece of card, and inside the square draw a circle which exactly touches all four sides. From time to time place the card on the floor and throw coins in its general direction. Keep a tally of the coins which fall inside the circle (I) and of those which fall inside the square but outside the circle (O). π = 4 × I ÷ (I + O). The calculated value of π should become more accurate as more coins are thrown.
Seán Kelly, London W7.

☐ A REMARKABLE approximation by Srinivasa Ramanujan in 1914 is π = the square root of the square root of 2143/22, which gives an accuracy to eight decimal places.
Geoff Wilkins, Handsworth, Birmingham.

QUESTION: Do wasps make honey?

☐ NO. Wasps *steal* honey in large amounts if they can get access to a bee-hive but usually they are carnivores, feeding on larvae and small insects. They have powerful jaws to chew up chitinous insects. A most unpleasant sight is to see a wasp neatly cut a honey bee in half and fly away with the abdomen section, leaving the poor bee's head and thorax still alive and walking about. Wasps do not in fact store anything. Their paper-like combs are only used to rear wasp larvae.

David S. Chadwick (entomologist), Fron Haul Apiaries, Anglesey, Gwynedd.

QUESTION: Don McLean wrote the song 'American Pie' as a tribute to Buddy Holly. The lyrics are enigmatic and seem loaded with allusions. What do they mean?

☐ AS WITH many other allusive pieces of writing, like *The Waste Land*, the effect is more to do with the creation of atmosphere, evoking several images at the same time, than a simple 'a-means-b' relationship. However, a few things can be said with assurance. The most important thing to remember is that the song isn't simply about the death of Buddy Holly, although that is certainly the theme of the first verse. After that, the song offers a chronological account of American youth throughout the sixties, focusing on the latter years of that decade. There are several references to specific individuals, some more obvious than others. So, for instance, the Jester is Bob Dylan, the line 'with the Jester on the sidelines in a cast' a reference to the motorcycle accident that temporarily halted his career. The King is Elvis Presley (of course), the Queen I'm not sure about. The Quartet are the Beatles, hence the previous line's 'while Lenin read a book on Marx' (McLean pronounces Lenin as 'Lennon') and the park is Candlestick Park, San Francisco, where they played their last live concert (another 'day the music died'). Jack Flash, unsurprisingly, is Mick Jagger, as is the 'Satan' (an allusion to the Stones' 'Sympathy for the Devil') later on in the verse, which seems to deal with the Altamont concert, where the group's Hell's Angel bodyguards (hence 'no angel born in hell/Could break that Satan's spell') stabbed to death a young black concert-goer named Meredith Hunter. 'A girl who sang the blues' is Janis Joplin, and 'The Father, Son and Holy Ghost' refers both to the three singers who died on Buddy Holly's plane (Holly himself, Richie Valens

and J P Richardson, the Big Bopper) and to the three most prominent assassination victims of the sixties, Martin Luther King, Bobby Kennedy and JFK. The song's non-musical allusions are rather less straightforward. However, I would say that it alludes to events including the Charles Manson killings ('Helter Skelter/In a summer swelter' – the Beatles' 'Helter Skelter' was the song that inspired Manson's family), the Vietnam War ('the Sergeants played a marching tune' – a reference to Sergeant Barry Sadler's gung-ho 'Ballad of the Green Beret'), anti-war demonstrations, including the 1968 riots at the Democrats' Chicago convention ('The players tried to take the field/The marching band refused to yield'), and Woodstock ('there we were all in one place'). Overall then, 'American Pie' paints a picture of the sixties, linked by a number of 'days the music died' from Buddy Holly's death, the singer's teenage romance, Candlestick Park, Chicago 1968, Altamont to the decade's uncertain end. It's one of the first songs to deal with the death of Sixties optimism, and one of the most effective.
David Cottis, Cardiff

☐ THE NAME of the programme escapes me, but the conversation followed these lines: Interviewer: 'Don, the song has been a bestseller for years and is now studied in university courses, so what does it really mean?' Don: 'It means that I don't have to work unless I want to.'
Gus Stewart, Hanwell, London W7.

QUESTION: At school we used to recite a mock Latin poem which began: 'Caesar adsum iam forte / Brutus aderat / Caesar sic in omnibus . . .' How did the poem end, and are there any more such joke Latin poems?

☐ 'BRUTUS sic inat'. According to Nigel Molesworth (1953), 'all latin masters hav one joke' and that's it. Molesworth also

notes that 'a good roare of larffter will cut the leson by two minits six seconds or half a gender rhyme'.
Peter Barnes, Milton Keynes.

☐ CAESAR carri donna militari orgi versus Belgao, Helvetii, Venetii, Britanni − iunemit. 'Romis glorius,' sed Caesar, 'Nomen me impunit'. Meni tridit, Veringetorix, forin stans; Caesar noctim sili fors ticinis nec aut. Ab ludi nervi felo, Caius Julius, iubet.
Elizabeth L Colquhoun, Huddersfield.

☐ CIVILE, se ergo, fortibuses in ero. Gnoses mare, thebe trux. Vatis in em, causan dux.
D. W. Larder, Chorley, Lancs.

☐ ONE morning, about 1933, someone brought into school a copy of the *Bootle Times* which contained a piece about the local find of an ancient Roman pot. Around the rim could be faintly discerned the words 'ITI SAPIS POTANDA BIGONE'. A local professor said that the Latin was somewhat corrupt but his rough translation included references to 'wisdom' and 'drinking'. I can't now remember when this hoax was first perpetrated but the *Bootle Times* was only one in a long line of victims.
W. F. Mullan, Nottingham.

QUESTION: Is there any scientific explanation for the phenomenon known as 'speaking in tongues'?

☐ RECENT research by a Montreal-based neurolinguist, Andre Roch Lecours, involved recording the 'xenoglossic' speech of a number of pentecostal charismatics and of a 'schizophasic' who believed he was the 'instrument of malevolent wills from Mars, where he once worked as a crooner.' It emerged that the phonetic elements of the 'alien' speech were virtually all to be found in the speakers' native language, with a smattering of sounds from languages of which they had a little passive knowledge. The 'alien language' also stuck pretty much to the other conventions of the native language's sound system, although often simplified in form. And though it appeared to include word- and sentence-like entities, such speech was marked by very simple transformational rules, considerable repetition, and an emphasis on rhythm and melody – as in more common monologue forms such as recitative prayer or political propaganda. A French neuropsychologist has reported how an English woman, who claimed to be a conduit for 'Pharaonic Egyptian', in fact drew from the repertoire of English sounds and euphonic principles such as alliteration – which would require a degree of self-control. Lecours suggests that 'speaking in tongues' is a 'learned game – and a rather simple one at that', which is based on making fluent utterances but with the semantic component switched off. Lecours' study had also included two healthy nurses and a professional poet, who were able to respond to the request to try to speak in a language they did not know by producing much the same kind of material. Furthermore, although the charismatics and the schizophasic claimed to be the instrument of some stronger will, they all produced on demand for recording. Flubbadub.

G. P. Collis, Liverpool 18.

□ A PAPERBACK, *The Psychology of Speaking in Tongues*, by John Kildahl, published in 1972, provides what is described as 'a scientific account' in simple terms.

(Revd) Michael Westney, Slough.

QUESTION: I'm sure I read somewhere that a BBC Repertory Company actor stood in for Winston Churchill to deliver some of his wartime speeches. If true, what was the reason?

☐ THE late Norman Shelley, the popular BBC *Children's Hour* actor (*Toytown*, etc.), told me he was called upon several times to perform this function – for example on June 4, 1940 ('We shall fight on the beaches'). Having made the speech once in the House that day, Winston, who loathed broadcasting, was unwilling or, some say, unable to make it again that night on the radio. Several times in 1940 millions of radio listeners were tricked into believing they were hearing Churchill's voice. I confirmed the story with Shelley for my biography, *Churchill's War* (Arrow Books); when Martin Gilbert, the other Churchill biographer, pooh-poohed it, I double-checked the BBC archives and, lo and behold, those were the only Churchill speeches for which there was no signed broadcasting contract. His desk diary also omits mention of any broadcast appointment on those evenings.
David Irving, London W1.

☐ AT REGULAR intervals during the war, Churchill would come to Broadcasting House to speak to the nation. He would bring with him his own scripts, which are still in the BBC's possession with his own handwritten annotations on them. In June, 1940, the British Council asked him to record a speech he made in the House of Commons on June 4, to be sent to the US to encourage support and sympathy. It is not surprising that there is no contract in the BBC files; this was a parliamentary speech and was not recorded or broadcast. He was obviously too busy at the time of the fall of France to come in and record for the British Council and said he would not object to an actor doing the recording for him, as long as he could hear it first. Norman Shelley was chosen and told the story in a women's magazine just before he died of going to meet Churchill and reading the speech to him. Then Churchill was able to hear the recording before it was sent to the US. The recording was made at the old Transcription Service Studios near Regent's Park. It wasn't really an 'impersonation', simply an actor reading in Churchill's style. Many in the US thought that it was the voice of Churchill himself. As a result of the article several myths have arisen. It has now even been suggested that most of Churchill's war broadcasts were made by Shelley. Here in the Archive we have watched this story grow with great interest and some irritation. However, Churchill did record this speech together with other parliamentary speeches in 1949 for the Decca 12 record set.

Sally K. Hine, BBC Sound Archives, Broadcasting House, London W1.

☐ THE ANSWER given by Sally Hine was irritating in the extreme. She states in her reply 'It wasn't really an impersonation' but simply an actor reading in the Churchill style. Can she tell me the difference? Or am I a bit thick? It wasn't only the people in the US who thought it was Churchill speaking. The whole of Great Britain was under the impression that it was Churchill. I was uplifted by the 1940 speech as never before or since and I can now understand my disappointment when I heard the 1949 recording in the *World at War*. It was an actor who had impressed me, albeit with Churchillian words.

G. M. Mackay, Orpington, Kent.

QUESTION: Is it true that if you throw a pea off the Eiffel Tower it can kill someone below?

☐ ONLY if it's in a tin.
Jacqueline Dunn, Manchester.

☐ FOR a light object like a pea to cause injury, it would need to be travelling as fast as a slow bullet – say 40 metres per second. There are two reasons why this speed would not be achieved. First, a fresh or canned pea would break up in the air before it reached that speed because of the force of wind resistance. This is easily observed if a canned pea is blown from a pea-shooter: it often breaks apart shortly after leaving the muzzle even though its speed is much lower than 40 metres per second. Secondly, even a dried pea will continue to accelerate only so long as its weight (the downward force) exceeds the air resistance (the upward force). All falling objects reach a speed where these two forces are equal and no further acceleration will take place. This is called the 'terminal velocity' and it is determined by the weight of the object, its shape, its surface characteristics and the temperature of the air. If we assume that a dried pea is 7mm diameter, weighs 400mg and is of 'moderate' smoothness, then in still air its terminal velocity is likely to be about nine metres per second. Being dried, it will probably not break up. At this velocity, the pea would be felt on the top of the head with an impulse equivalent to a new 5p coin dropped from about 600 millimetres. No injury would result. However, a hard smooth sea-pebble of the same size could reach a terminal velocity of about 50 metres per second and could injure.

Vic Seddon, Teesside Polytechnic.

QUESTION: What is the origin of the silent 'b' at the end of English words such as lamb, comb, crumb and bomb?

☐ WE OWE the silent 'b' to the fact that centuries ago our ancestors pronounced a b-sound: climb was Old English climban, and bomb comes from Italian *bomba*. The b-sound was lost by about 1300. It leaves traces to the present day, however, in pairs such as climb-clamber, crumb-crumble. Thumb appears to be a rogue case, because here the 'b' is not etymological; there may have been influence from thimble. There are about 20 words in ending in 'mb'. In some of the rarer ones, such as lamb or coulomb, people sometimes pronounce a b-sound. Phonetically, 'b' is classified as a voiced plosive, as are 'd' and 'g'. Sound changes applying to one tend to apply to the other two as well. This is so with 'g' for those among us who pronounce no g-sound after the nasal at the end of sing and hang, but not for those mid-landers and northerners who make singer rhyme with finger. But 'd' remains in the standard pronunciation of mind, stand, round (perhaps because we need the 'nd' sequence of sounds to keep the past tense distinct from the present in fined, tanned, crowned). Even so, we readily omit the 'd' in speech in phrases like mind the doors, stand back, round the corner.

J. C. Wells, Professor of Phonetics, University of London.

QUESTION: Why don't airliners supply parachutes to passengers?

☐ THIS was a live issue during the Second World War when small fighter aircraft, such as the Spitfire, were considered more valuable than the pilots who flew them. The argument ran along the lines of balancing the number of planes lost because their pilots baled out unnecessarily, against the shortage of trained pilots that would occur if they were not given the chance to escape. Today's airline passengers are not fighting for their country, so it would be bad business to save them in the event of an (most unlikely) enemy attack. There are plenty more willing and paying customers who know full well that 'in the unlikely event of a plane having to put down on water' they don't stand a chance of surviving the impact. Since it is during the take-off or landing manoeuvres that 98 per cent of all airline accidents occur, the odds of any passengers saving themselves by jumping out of the plane clutching parachutes are incredibly slim. It

is much more pertinent to demand safety belts on trains and buses.
Patrick C. Graham, Cardiff.

☐ IT IS MOST unlikely that a parachute will be of use if a passenger plane crashes. Even a plane-load of active military parachutists takes several minutes of reasonably steady flight to exit. Parachuting takes nerve, skill, and strength. One has to force oneself into a 150 mph slipstream, hold a posture that stops one tangling with the parachute as it opens, steer clear of one's fellows and land safely. I shudder to think what the casualty list would be if a typical group of passengers were to attempt their first descents in an emergency. The average man, woman or child in a Boeing would stand a better chance of survival riding the plane down.
D. Waterton, Wigan, Lancs.

☐ AS IT takes several minutes to don a parachute, passengers would have to wear one throughout the flight – uncomfortable and impractical, especially on long-haul journeys. Accidental deployment of a canopy would have dire consequences, especially on the plane's stability if dragged out of an open door with the passenger still strapped in his/her seat. The G-forces of a crashing plane are immense. A plane needs to slow to about 70 mph otherwise a jumper could end up wrapped around the tail-plane. Also, the harness might damage or hinder the pneumatic escape chutes, if used in a ground emergency.
Phil Edwards, (member of the British Parachute Association), Crewe, Cheshire.

☐ SOME of the answers are slightly erroneous or incomplete. It is true that at times early in the war, we had a shortage of Spitfire and Hurricane pilots, but for many years before that, all our fighter pilots had parachutes – and as our pilots knew that Luftwaffe pilots had parachutes, the psychological effect of even seriously considering parachuteless Battle of Britain pilots would have been devastating. However, the concept of pilots baling out unnecessarily did influence both sides to withhold parachutes in the Great War, although towards its end some German pilots were given parachutes. As for airliners, an early reason for no parachutes was that the public would have considered the first airline to provide them for passengers to be using unsafe aircraft (otherwise, why supply parachutes?). Another strong reason was cost and weight, for a feasible system suggested before the war, when air navigation was less exact and engines less reliable, was for each passenger seat to include a parachute, each whole seat and passenger being dropped through the cabin floor, in sequence from the rear. But quite apart from the huge weight penalty, what if the sequencing mechanism accidentally operated while the airliner was just taking off? In any case, modern jetliners travel so fast even when in trouble, that most passengers would be killed just stepping outside, by the battering airflow.

Len Clarke (ex-military and civil pilot), Uxbridge, Middx.

QUESTION: 'Tie a yellow ribbon round the old oak tree.' Why yellow?

☐ DURING the American Civil War, Union soldiers were given the nickname 'yellow legs' by their confederate counterparts. The name referred to the uniform, with obvious derisory overtones. Mothers, wives, sisters and daughters of Union soldiers took to wearing yellow flowers (roses in particular) as a rebuke to this slander and to show solidarity with their menfolk. The yellow ribbon is a direct descendant of this.

Thomas Boyce, Doha, Qatar.

☐ THOMAS BOYCE comes close, but is not exact. Yellow was the distinguishing colour of the US cavalry since its official formation in March 1833, the colour of the trouser stripe

and also of NCO's chevrons and of piping on shell jacket or
cap. It was not restricted to the Civil War, and it did not
apply to all Union soldiers: the Artillery wore red stripes and
pipes, and the Infantry varied but never wore yellow. Mr
Boyce mentions 'mothers, wives sisters and daughters', but
omits the most important category who in her hair 'would
wear a yellow ribbon; would wear it in the springtime, in the
merry month of May . . .'
Gordon Medcalf, Reading, Berks.

☐ IT MAY be true that there is a link between yellow flowers
and the Civil War, but there seems to have been no link with
yellow ribbons. According to an article in *The Express*
(Berkeley, California), yellow ribbons were first used in
January 1981, to welcome home the Americans held hostage
in Iran. The inspiration was the song, 'Tie a Yellow Ribbon
Round the Old Oak Tree', although that had been written in
1972 and is about a convict returning home from jail. Even
more confusing is that Larry Brown, one of the writers,
claimed the centrepiece of the story on which he based the
song was a white kerchief. He changed this to 'yellow
ribbon' to scan better. There had been previous songs about
yellow ribbons, such as 'She Wore a Yellow Ribbon' (title for
the 1949 John Ford movie), but these cannot be traced back
to the real, rather than the Hollywood, Civil War.
Richard Ross, London N4.

☐ ABOUT a year before the song was inflicted upon us I saw a
short drama on American television that began on an overnight coach crossing America. One of the passengers has just
got out of jail, is on his way home and doesn't know if his
wife wants him back, but he has asked her to show him a
sign (the colour was yellow simply because it was their
favourite). The next morning, as the coach nears his home,
all the passengers stare eagerly out of the windows to see if
the ribbon is there . . . and the last shot of the film is the ex-

con standing on his front lawn, staring up at the tree, festooned with ribbons.
Adam Kimmel, London N7.

QUESTION: When did the expression 'Russian roulette' first come into use? Why Russian? Are there authenticated cases of it being played?

☐ RUSSIAN roulette may have its origins in *A Hero of Our Time* by Mikhail Lermontov (1814–41) where he tells of a Lieutenant Vulich whose only passion was for cards, where he usually lost – and most of his money at that. When an argument arose about predestination, he maintained there was no such thing and backed his belief with a wager of 200 roubles. He was taken up on the bet whereupon he walked to a wall with weapons hanging on it and at random took one of the pistols. He poured powder into the touch-pan and asked the pistol's owner – a major – if the pistol was loaded. The owner didn't remember. Vulich held the pistol to his head and pulled the trigger. It misfired. Some of the onlookers said it wasn't loaded. Vulich cocked the gun again, aimed at a cap hanging over the window and a bullet pierced its centre.
S. Kaufman, Ilford, Essex.

☐ THERE is a wealth of fictional references, notably the 19th-century Russian writer, Ossendowski, in his unforgettable *Man and Mystery in Asia*. But the most well-documented factual example is surely Graham Greene's experience of at least six episodes. One took place (summer 1924–January 1925) while he was up at Oxford: 'I would walk out from Headington towards Elsfield . . . a sodden unfrequented country lane; the revolver would be whipped behind my back, the chamber twisted, the muzzle quickly inserted in my ear beneath the black winter trees, the trigger pulled . . .' Evidence was left behind in the form of free verse

permanently on his desk 'so that if I lost the gamble, it would provide in controvertible evidence of an accident, and my parents, I thought, would be less troubled by a fatal play-acting than a suicide'.
John Bray, Haywards Heath, W Sussex.

QUESTION: Why is Parmesan cheese at least three times as expensive as any other cheese?

☐ PARMESAN needs significantly more milk than other cheese (16 litres to make one kilogram). As with any product that matures slowly, the price is commensurate with the stage of its maturity. Twelve months is the minimum time before a Parmesan cheese is allowed by law to leave the factory and then it is categorised (and priced) by its maturity: vecchio (old), stravecchio (extra or very old), tipico (four to five years) and giovane (young). The manufacturing process still uses certain traditional methods, and this is also reflected in the eventual price. It's interesting to note that Parmesan is reputed to have medicinal qualities. Doctors in the production region often prescribe it to children with intestinal problems, and if its claimed aphrodisiacal properties get you into trouble you can always take comfort in the fact that the skin of a good 'vecchio' is practically bullet-proof.
Derek Rose and Renato Grotti, Luxembourg.

QUESTION: Why are pirates invariably depicted with eyepatches and wooden legs? Was there a higher incidence of industrial injury in their line of work, or were they just clumsy?

☐ THERE was a high rate of such industrial injuries in all sea-faring between the middle of the 17th century and the end of the Napoleonic wars (the period featured in Holly-

wood swashbucklers). It could hardly have been otherwise. The most common form of sea engagement during that period seems to have been the medium or close-range firing of cannon broadside on, at, or between, vessels. On to and into those ships came smashing cannon balls, which, when they did not decapitate or otherwise kill outright, lopped off limbs, or at least smashed them so destructively the only known chance for survival was prompt amputation. Cannonades brought down heavy timber on and through decks – more crushing injuries, more amputations – and turned the wood of a ship into cutting projectiles. If muskets were used at closer range, a heavy musket-ball was at least as likely to smash a limb (needing amputation) as to pierce it. And in hand-to-hand combat to secure a ship, the cutlass was common, because as a slashing weapon it could be used with the minimum of footwork, in tight conditions. More severing injuries, and also vertical cuts to the forehead and down through the eye-area. Although soldiers during the same era faced similar dangers, the concentration of fire on the relatively small, man-filled target of a ship must have meant sailors/pirates had a very high chance of mutilation. An even bigger one of death. And at sea it isn't easy to run away.
Ann MacDonald, Clapham, London.

☐ THE MAIN cause, surely, was the type of artillery in use. Eighteenth-century cannons were loaded with coarse black gunpowder, and fired by putting some of the powder in a hole at the back of the gun and lighting it with a slow match. Although most of the powder would blast forward, an appreciable proportion would vent out through the touchhole. Anyone firing a cannon was therefore very likely to get a blast of burning powder in the face, with a grave risk of eye injury. A smooth-bored gun, firing a roughly rounded shot with poor quality powder from a moving ship would only have an accurate range of a few yards. It was probably customary to fire a broadside practically at the point of contact. At that range a cannonball fired into the side of a

wooden ship would scatter large jagged splinters of wood about the deck. Anyone receiving a wound in the body would probably die of gangrene within a few days. Gangrene could be prevented in a limb injury, however, by rapid removal of the limb (first partially anaesthetising the patient with rum or laudanum – a solution of opium and rum), tying up the cut arteries and cauterising the stump in hot tar. Anyone who survived the immediate traumatic effect of this treatment would probably escape gangrenous infection, but would have to make use of a prosthetic device such as a hook or wooden leg.
Martin Guha, London SE3.

☐ ONCE you've got a shiny new hook for a hand you'll discover why an eye patch is needed when you attempt to rub your eye.
Bridget Savage, Bexley, Kent.

☐ SAILORS of the period who were injured were discharged. As their trade was the sea, their only recourse to earn a living was piracy. Their physical disabilities were an advantage if they instilled fear into their unfortunate victims: the more ruthless they appeared, the greater their chance of success.
F. E. Jones, Gt Sankey, Warrington.

QUESTION: I live in a house built in the 1860s and the ceilings are about 10 ft high. The rooms must have been twice as difficult to heat as they are today. Why did they build them so high?

☐ THE JUSTIFICATION is to be found in Roman/Greek architecture and the social attitudes of our forefathers. The 1860s witnessed the creation of industrial wealth – coupled with squalor for many of the working classes. Habitation for the poor generally consisted of hovels with low ceilings, bad ventilation and almost non-existent public sewerage. The idea that bad health and therefore life expectancy was

directly attributable to the quality of the 'airs' was evident to those who endured or witnessed these conditions. The 1870s subsequently gave rise to legislation which resulted in the Building Bye-Laws. By comparison, those who could afford better conditions plumped for classically inspired architecture, its roots in the Mediterranean, with all those associations with the health-promoting quality of its climate. The principal expression of the classical style which we call Georgian was followed notably by the Greek Revival School. The basis of all classical architecture is a heavy dependence on the rules of proportion and geometrical relationships. It was considered that the most satisfying proportion for a principal room or salon was that based on the double cube (that is height = breadth: 2 × height or breadth = length). These proportions are to be seen in most of our stately homes. The builders of many of our Victorian residences had to compromise on these proportions, and as 10ft is the smallest practical dimension for a lounge, the length was reduced – the height remained unchanged. Thus many Victorian drawing rooms are frequently 16–18ft long by 10ft wide and high, representing a reasonable economic compromise in space terms and airiness. The speculative builder of the late 19th century was selling good health at a time when life expectancy was not great.
H. Stevenson, Bramhall, Cheshire.

□ DOMESTIC lighting in the 1860s was commonly from 'bats wing' gas burners which are said to have given off smoky, smelly fumes. Ceilings were made high so that the fumes would not to bother people below.
Anthony McMahon, London NW5.

□ EACH year this problem is discussed by thousands of GCE physics students when they study 'energy in buildings'. The reason for high ceilings in older buildings is to allow daylight to penetrate deep into the interior. Whether conditions are clear or overcast, most of the light entering a window is coming from the sky. After passing through the glass it continues on its downward gradient into the room. The higher the top of the window, the further back the light reaches. The ratio of the height of the top of the window to the depth of the room thus determines how well illuminated the room is. Neither candles, oil lamps, nor gas lamps could produce light anywhere near as bright as daylight, without using huge amounts of energy and producing large amounts of heat and fumes. Thus, before electric light, many indoor activities had to be performed by daylight. The higher the ceilings and windows, the longer into the evening, and the more comfortably, the activities could be performed. Early electric lamps and early electricity generation and distribution systems were not as efficient as their modern counterparts. Thus even after the first electric lights, the cost of electricity saved by high windows, allowing in more daylight, was greater than the cost of the extra heating needed. When the relative cost of lighting and heating reversed, ceilings became lower to reduce construction and heating costs, and daylight was regularly supplemented with electric lighting. Now that we are more concerned about the financial and environmental costs of all energy use, the appearance of buildings is changing again. We can now design to give minimum energy losses and the maximum exploitation of solar energy for lighting and heating, without producing excessive summer solar gain.

Steve Bolter, Braintree College, Essex.

QUESTION: I once read a nonsense poem that removed the apparently negative prefixes of words like 'inept', 'inert' and 'uncouth' to make new words: 'ept', 'ert' and 'couth'. I've searched for the poem since, but no luck. Can anyone help?

☐ THE POEM to which I think the question refers is 'Gloss' by an American poet, David McCord, which runs:

I know a little man both ept and ert.
An intro? extro? No, he's just a vert.
Shevelled and couth and kempt, pecunious, ane.
His image trudes upon the ceptive brain.
When life turns sipid and the mind is traught,
The spirit soars as I would sist it ought.
Chalantly then, like any gainly goof,
My digent self is sertive choate, loof.

I hope this is of sistance.
J D Trehearne, Ealing, London W5.

☐ THE POEM is probably:
I dreamt of a corrigible nocuous youth,
Gainly, gruntled and kempt;
A mayed and sidious fellow forsooth –
Ordinate, effable, shevelled, ept, couth;
A delible fellow I dreamt.

Quoted by Willard R Espy in his book, *The Game of Words*
(Bramhall House, New York).
C Sherris, Billingham, Cleveland.

QUESTION: Why do gentlemen prefer blondes?

☐ ALTHOUGH the word 'gentlemen' is written above more
than half the public lavatories in Britain, most of those who
go there are serfs, villeins, churls or at best, franklins or
yeomen. Gentlemen are the lowest grade of the aristocracy.
Since early medieval times, members of the aristocracy have
been of Scandinavian origin. They started off as the henchmen of Eric Bloodaxe or Canute, and later additions were
the henchmen of William the Conqueror, who was not a
Frenchman but the descendant of Norsemen (or Norwe-
gians, or Normans) who took over part of France. So both
genuine gentlemen and social climbers of mere Celtic
ancestry seek out glamorous, powerful and above all yellow-
haired descendants of Scandinavian overlords.
John Ward, Bristol.

☐ IN CHEMISTS' shops and supermarkets row after row of shelves are assigned to a wide range of DIY dye kits, blonde being the bestseller. This leads me to the conclusion that in fact it is women and not gentlemen who prefer blondes.
Tom Williams, Stockport.

☐ ANITA LOOS (the author of *Gentlemen Prefer Blondes*) was asked in an interview in, I think, the 1970s, what she would call the book if it were updated. She replied: 'Gentlemen Prefer Gentlemen'.
George Moore, London SW2.

QUESTION: Despite many years' experience teaching English as a foreign language, I have never been able to answer the question 'What is the difference between jam and marmalade?' Can anyone help?

☐ THERE is no difference: marmalade is yellow jam. The marmalade has its origins in the Greek *mel* meaning honey, which passed into Latin as *melimelon*, and then to the Portuguese *marmalada* from the word *marmelo* meaning quince. This quince jam called *marmelada* is still very popular in Portugal and became *marmelade* in the French. Marmalade is a yellow jam and has passed into the English language as such, though oranges and lemons are now used in place of quince.
Kristine Byrne, Lagos, Portugal.

☐ TO SAY that marmalade is yellow jam ignores the use of citrus fruit, particularly Seville oranges, surely essential to any definition of marmalade (ginger marmalade being the exception that proves the rule). This semantic difference between the words comes from their history. 'Marmalade' does derive from the Latin for quince via Portuguese; quince paste, or *marmelada* was a luxury imported from Portugal to England in the 16th century. Over the following century 'marmalade' was applied to pastes made from sugar and many kinds of fruit: peaches, damsons, oranges and lemons, as well as quinces; some recipes used almonds. The pastes were stiff and cut in slices to eat from the fingers; softer pastes with a higher water content simply didn't keep. 'Jam' entered the English language in the 18th century, making an early appearance in Mrs Mary Eales' *Receipts* (1718). It may derive from an Arabic word meaning 'to pack together'. Improved hygiene led to the development of runnier marmalades, similar to jam as we know it today. By 1861, Mrs Beeton stated that 'Marmalades and jams differ little from each other: they are preserves of half liquid consistency made by boiling the pulp of fruits and sometimes the rinds with sugar', with the proviso that marmalades were made from firm fruits, such as pineapples or the rinds of oranges; jams were made from soft fruit. For reasons which are not entirely obvious, the name marmalade stuck to orange preserves, while the more downwardly mobile fruit spreads were lumped together as jam. No doubt the EC will soon settle the argument for once and all with a directive on the subject. A fuller discussion of the history of marmalade is provided by C. Anne Wilson in *A Book of Marmalade* (1985).

Laura Mason, York.

☐ I SUGGEST we haul ourselves out of the morass of etymology and remember that language is a tool for naming things. In which case, for 99.9 per cent of the British, marmalade is made of oranges (or more rarely other citrus fruits) while jam is made of any non-citrus fruit. The 0.1 per cent also mess with things like turnips and rhubarb – these concoctions are called jam too.

John Stagg, London NW11.

QUESTION: Why is it that when a bluebottle flies towards a window, it hits the glass with tremendous force and yet does not kill itself?

☐ IT DOES not hit the window with tremendous *force*, but with (relatively) tremendous *speed*. The elementary definition of force in Newton's mechanics is: $F = m \times a$ where m is the mass of the moving object and a is its acceleration. In the case of the bluebottle, the factor a, produced by its travelling at speed, then coming to rest at the instant of collision, is quite large; but the mass of the bluebottle is very small indeed. Therefore, though the collision happens at high speed, the force it produces on the bluebottle is really quite small, certainly not enough to harm it. A human, for example, hitting the window at the same speed would do itself – and the window – considerably more damage.
John Delaney, London SE25.

☐ IT APPEARS that the flies smeared across the windscreen of my car (a not-so-speedy 2CV) had not read John Delaney's answer. Can anyone provide a more concise answer to the crumple velocity of these insects?
Chris James, Coventry.

QUESTION: What is the origin of the word 'hijack'?

☐ IT ORIGINATES from the prohibition era in America. Supposedly a member of one gang would approach the driver of a rival gang's bootlegging truck with a smile and a disarming 'Hi, Jack!' before sticking the muzzle of a gat in the face of the poor unfortunate, and relieving him of both truck and its alcoholic cargo.
Tim Wood, Cardiff.

☐ THE word 'hijack' has its origins in pre-revolutionary

France. Impoverished peasants attacked and robbed aristocrats travelling in coaches through the countryside. The word they employed for this practice was 'échaquer', which, sharing a common root with 'éjecter' in the Latin word 'eiacere', meant primarily the physical removal of the aristocrat from his carriage and of his possessions from his person, but also, through its onomatopoeic second syllable, contained elements of the peasants' anger, expressed in the guttural spitting sound used to pronounce the word and also possibly the sound of a knife entering and twisting up through the aristocrat's intestines. Wider implications of the word were explored in the revolution of 1789. The word reached England by way of the many English bandits who worked alongside their French colleagues. The reason for this was similar in many ways to the situation today where unemployed Englishmen pick grapes in France. In the 18th century the pickings were simply richer in France. The aristocrats were vain and haughty and felt themselves to be untouchable. This made it a simple matter to relieve them of their considerable wealth. I do not know whether the word was misheard as 'é Jacques' and thus translated by the English brigands as 'i Jack' or if the word was taken as heard and, due to the similarity in 18th-century rural English pronunciation between the 'e' and 'i' sounds, has simply come to be written down as 'hijack' by adding the 'h' an educated person of that time would have assumed a peasant to have left off. The word 'échaquer' disappeared from French usage after the revolution. Today, the French use the word 'détourner' which, in its mildness, perhaps best sums up the civilising influence of the revolution. It also reflects the changing usage of the word 'hijack' which today refers almost exclusively to the taking over by force of an aeroplane or other vehicle by a group of terrorists who wish it to go to a different destination. Thus the French have a new word for a word which originated in their own language.

Peter Bowen, London SW12.

QUESTION: What is the irritating eight-bar theme that interrupts my evening radio listening, especially winter Test Match specials? From which European station is it broadcast ?

☐ THIS haunting phrase is the beginning of the Albanian national patriotic march, 'With Pickaxe and Rifle', played on two trumpets, and is the interval signal of Radio Tirana. Without doubt it is the most assertive interval signal of any radio station (the least assertive must be Radio Vatican City, which uses the sound of doves cooing). It is not the only music Tirana's listeners are treated to; I remember once hearing a catchy little number called 'We March Through the Five-Year Plan'. I have never tracked down the rest of 'With Pickaxe and Rifle' but it occurs to me that the first phrase of the British national patriotic march, 'Land of Hope and Glory', played in the same way and endlessly repeated would not only be just as annoying but eerily similar into the bargain.

V. W. Cappaert, South Ockendon, Essex.

☐ THE 1215 kHz channel was assigned to Albania as well as Britain in the 1975 Long Wave and Medium Wave plan agreed by the International Frequency Registration Board. The frequency has a 500 kW transmitter at Lushnje (19deg 40 E, 40deg 57 N) and is used for overseas broadcasting. Anyone wishing to hear the station broadcasting in English can tune in on another medium wave channel, 1395 kHz at 2230 GMT (2330 BST).

S. N. J. Spanswick, Assistant Secretary-General, European DX Council, London SE3.

□ THE clearly audible broadcasts from Radio Tirana have been a thorn in the BBC's flesh for many years, which is one reason why they are handing over 1215 kHz for use by one of the new national commercial radio stations.
John Mann, Banbury, Oxon.

□ UNTIL the recent changes in Albania, Radio Tirana's broadcasts in English were highly entertaining neo-Stalinist propaganda, with extracts from the latest volume of Comrade Enver Hoxha's speeches, and attacks on almost every country for being politically out of line. The presenters had flawless English pronunciation, but with very curious intonation, which led me to surmise that they were reading from a phonetic script and didn't actually understand the meaning. Every broadcast ended with 'Goodbye, dear listeners!' and a rousing version of the 'Internationale'. All has changed now, however. Last time I tuned in, it was all about what Albanians like to eat for Christmas dinner.
S. K. Lewicki, Leeds.

QUESTION: What is the origin of the phrase 'poisoned chalice'?

□ *MACBETH* (Act I, scene 7), dithering about whether or not to murder King Duncan, considers the possibility that his successful use of this technique might inspire imitators once he is himself king:

> . . . *we but teach*
> *Bloody instructions, which being taught return*
> *To plague th'inventor; this even-handed justice*
> *Commends th'ingredience of our poisoned chalice*
> *To our own lips.*

Anthea Jackson, Coxhoe, Durham.

□ IN the Middle Ages, feuding lords would often dispatch their enemies by offering a 'conciliatory' cup of wine which had been doctored with hemlock. Canny lords insisted on tipping a small portion of their drink into their new-found friend's chalice as a precaution. This is the origin of clinking our glasses together and wishing each other good health before downing the beverage.

Chris Wright, Hull, N Humberside.

☐ IF THIS has a definite origin it is not those given so far. There is a tradition, going back to the 3rd-century 'Acts of St John', that the enemies of the saint once tried to do away with him by offering him a poisoned chalice. Medieval depictions of St John consequently showed him holding a cup like a communion chalice (calix) with a serpent wrapped round it. It is almost certainly this image which gave the phrase its currency.

C V Gidlow, Faversham, Kent.

QUESTION: The round trip to my bottle bank is five miles. My car, on unleaded petrol, averages 30 miles per gallon under urban driving conditions. How many bottles do I need to take to make the journey ecologically defensible?

☐ IF THE questioner used his car for nothing but journeys to the bottle bank, then the journeys would cost garaging, road tax, depreciation, insurance, breakdown membership, servicing, repairs, petrol, oil, batteries, tyres, cleaners, polishes, etc, several hundred pounds. If, however, he spreads the cost over an average mileage of 1,000 miles per month, the cost might be about 50p per mile, i.e. £5 for the bottle bank journey. With glass at about £30 per ton and bottles weighing about 1lb each and 2240lbs in a ton, £5 would be the price realised for about 400 bottles.

Bryn Jones, Welwyn Garden City, Herts.

☐ IT IS the view of the glass industry that people should not waste energy making special journeys, but that they should incorporate their visit to the bottle bank with a specific journey i.e., a trip to the supermarket.

National Recycling Manager, United Glass, St Albans, Herts.

☐ BRYN JONES'S estimate could condemn a lot of innocent bottles to an environmentally unfriendly end. His figure of 50p per mile covers all motoring costs from petrol to road tax and depreciation. But the only costs relevant to the bank-or-bin decision are the marginal ones of petrol, servicing, wear on tyres, etc. Costs such as road tax are constant, irrespective of usage, and can be ignored for this purpose. On AA figures this marginal cost is 17p per mile for an average car (of which 8p is petrol) so the marginal cost of the 10-mile trip is £1.70. It would be justified by 130 bottles, not 400. However this still ducks the real issue of how to put a price on the environment, since only the market costs visibly incurred are being considered. The long-term social costs could be very different, though not so easy to deal with. What about the 10 miles' worth of carbon dioxide contributed to the greenhouse effect? Or the cost of disposing acceptably of worn-out tyres? Not to mention additional pressure on limited road space, and noise pollution.

Martin Bennett, Ashridge Management College, Berkhamsted, Herts.

QUESTION: I have recently started getting electric shocks when I get out and lock my car after driving it. Why, and what can I do to stop it?

☐ THE CHARGE is worse in dry weather and is related to the conductivity of the tyres. I suspect the questioner has recently changed one or more tyres to a brand which, although better from a wear and roadholding aspect, is a bad conductor. As static can be blamed for shocks, car

sickness, fire and complete ruination of AM car radio reception, it seems strange that the PR people have not made a feature of it rather than the doubtful advantages of taking your breath away.
Alan Watling, Colchester

☐ FROM the fact that the questioner has only recently experienced this phenomenon, I would deduce that he has bought a new pair of shoes. The shock is the result of earthing through the car body of the electrostatic charge which has built up from the contact and friction of clothing and the fabric of the car's seats. With most shoes this charge leaks painlessly away to earth as soon as one's foot touches the pavement. But with some kinds of synthetic sole the charge is retained, and if I recall correctly my school physics, is concentrated at points, such as fingertips or key ends.
(Revd) Nicholas I Kerr, Sidcup, Kent.

☐ I PREVENT this by first washing the loose car-seat covers and then using fabric conditioner in the rinsing water.
(Mrs) E. R. Stout, Formby, Liverpool.

☐ I CURED the problem by purchasing one of those beaded seats. They're very comfortable and prevent static build-up.
P. M. Dodd, Longlevens, Gloucester.

☐ MAKE sure that your hand is in contact with the car bodywork *before* your feet touch the ground. There is thus no arcing and no shock is felt.
Peter Seddon, Litherland, Liverpool.

☐ AVOID touching any metal part while getting out of the car. Then, grasping the metal of your car key between finger and thumb, touch the lock with the key. You may see a spark, especially at night, but will feel no shock.
Dennis Kaye, Huddersfield.

☐ PERHAPS the questioner should look at buying a Mazda 323. We have recently introduced a face-lift version and one of its highlights is a special anti-static switch to stop this occurring. It is a very simple device and is operated by pressing a button at the top of the door.
Tim Watson, Public Relations Manager, Mazda Cars (UK) Ltd, Tunbridge Wells, Kent.

QUESTION: What is the source of the American expression: 'Between a rock and a hard place'?

☐ THIS seems to be an American update of 'between Scylla and Charybdis'. Scylla is a rock, a hazard to navigation, on the Italian side of the Straits of Messina. Facing it on the Sicilian side of the Straits is Charybdis, a dangerous whirlpool (now called Calofaro), and certainly 'a hard place'. Hence the sense of avoiding one unpleasantness only to fall foul of another. Shelley, to name but one, used it, as in 'between the Scylla and Charybdis of anarchy and despotism'.
Stewart McDiarmid, London SE4.

QUESTION: Why do French notebooks have squared rather than lined paper?

☐ THE vertical lines are to help children write straight individual letters. They also provide guide-lines to indent paragraphs and draw diagrams. Children are generally requested to use this squared paper until in higher education, where more freedom is granted and English-type ruled paper is very trendy. Another difference is that French children learn directly to join up letters and do not go through the intermediate stage of 'printing' them as is the practice in the UK.
Anne Leprince, London W1.

☐ THE FRENCH are taught handwriting from a very early age resulting in everyone having the same style. The squared paper enables the writer to form the letters more exactly. As to why this tradition began, I can only suggest that it might be a throwback to revolutionary times when the various governments seem to have tried to control all aspects of French life.
M J Taylor, Jesmond, Newcastle upon Tyne.

☐ IT'S BECAUSE the French use a graph accent. A cute idea, n'est-ce-pas?
Martin Fowkes, Oadby, Leicester.

IS THIS a question.

☐ NO, this is a demonstrative pronoun.
Bob Gingell, Coventry.

☐ STUDENT lore has it that this appeared on a University of London finals paper in philosophy in the 1950s, and that one attempted answer ran: 'If that is a question, this is an answer.' Legend records that the student in question failed,

but would have passed had he sat his finals in Oxford, where there is a greater tolerance of Smart Alecks.
Paul Richards.

☐ No, of course it isn't a question, because it doesn't have a question mark. But this grammatical lapse is compounded by a logical one. It isn't a question because although it conforms (with the addition of the question mark) to the way we normally formulate questions in our language, it contains a logical mistake. The similarly structured 'Is that a quintain?' is both perfectly structured and perfectly meaningful in an appropriate context. But 'Is this a question?' lacks any context in which it would be appropriate. It commits what is known by logicians as a 'type error' and is meaningless in the same way as the statement 'the average taxpayer died yesterday' is meaningless — and for similar reasons. The latter is nonsense because the sorts of things that can be done by 'the average taxpayer' do not include 'dying yesterday'. In our non-question, the 'this' refers circularly — and emptily — to itself. Compare 'Is that a question?' which is OK because the 'that' refers elsewhere. The sorts of things that a question can do may not include asking a question about itself. There are, inevitably, odd cases where questions can ask questions about elements, or aspects of themselves ('Does this question start with the word "does"?') But logic sensibly draws a firm line at circular vacuity.
(Dr) William Johnston, Arnside, Cumbria.

☐ I answer 'Yes', since to offer any answer at all is to concede that it is indeed a question. Objectors can offer only a silence after the four words are uttered: any response would confirm my view. Thus, I can receive no valid objection. 'Is this a question?' is framed in accordance with common English usage for questions (when correctly punctuated), and has received at least one answer. And so, if it walks like a duck and it quacks like a duck . . . I rest my case.

Bill Allen, Montrose Gardens, Oxshott, Surrey.

☐ Bob Gingell's error is to ignore the vital contribution that quotation marks make to meaning. Had the question been whether 'this' is a question (which it was not) then the correct answer would have been that 'this' is not a question but a demonstrative pronoun. Dr William Johnston's position is self-refuting: it provides an answer – albeit a false one – to what it denies is a question. Moreover, the details of his answer show that he understood very well the meaning of what he claims to be a meaningless non-question. If we are to banish otherwise perfectly well-formed sentences merely because they are self-referential, what are we to do with Shakespeare's 18th Sonnet? '. . . So long as men can breathe or eyes can see/So long lives this, and this gives life to thee.'

Moshace Machover, Reader in Mathematical Logic, Dept of History and Philosophy of Science, King's College, London.

☐ Compare Wittgenstein's 'This statement is false'.

Robin Howard, Haywards Heath, W Sussex.

☐ This is not an answer. But I recommend the full and highly entertaining discussion in chapters one and two of *Metamagical Themas* by Douglas R. Hofstadter which includes the classic 'This sentence no verb'.

Lesz Lancucki, London SW12.

☐ All these cunning answers are actually irrelevant because Shakespeare told us that 'that is the question'.

Michael Wilson, Wigton, Cumbria.

☐ This sentence no verb. Who cares. This reader bored. Time to bring this subject to a.

Christopher Turner, Sevenoaks, Kent.

QUESTION: Would I be right in thinking that the inter-woven braids of the maypole represent mankind's ear-liest attempt at a stored program?

☐ THE i ching predates the maypole by several centuries; the trigrams and hexagrams are pieces of information stored in a binary code of three or six 'bits'.
Gordon Joly, 14 Flora Close, London E14.

☐ IN SUGGESTING that the i ching is an earlier attempt, Gordon Joly confuses the idea of information stored in binary code with a program. Clearly, the interwoven braids of the maypole store the pattern of the dance and could be used to reproduce it. So we have a program.
Bill Cross, Northallerton, N Yorks.

☐ THE ARGUMENT against the i ching (c1150 BC) being a 'stored program' that predates the maypole dance observes that 'the interwoven braids . . . store the pattern of the dance'. This is similar to the pattern stored in DNA or a knitting pattern. DNA uses four bases, in pairs, labelled A, C, G, T to store the information to build a tree or a human. DNA therefore has the following binary codes, assigned arbitrarily: 00, 10, 01, 11. A modern definition of 'stored program' would certainly include the possibility of the inclusion of a 'conditional statement' (e.g., 'if A is true then do B else C'). It is not clear that the maypole pattern could have a conditional statement. However, in the i ching (Book of Changes) yarrow sticks or coins are cast, and the meaning of the resulting patterns is read from the full 64 (six-bit) hexagrams. There are some variations, but this is the basic principle. The i ching, as a stored program, is essentially used to read elements and energies in the universe at large. The notion of using chance events (compare reading tea leaves) to tell us something about complex future (or cur-

rent) events is also used in modern computing techniques such as neural networks, 'Monte Carlo' methods, and genetic algorithms.
Gordon Joly, London E14.

QUESTION: Does 'Don't cast a clout till May be out' refer to the bush or the month?

☐ IT PROBABLY refers to the month, although the may tree (whitethorn or hawthorn) is strongly associated with May, when it usually flowers. According to Robert Graves, in *The White Goddess*, the saying means 'do not put on new clothes until the unlucky month is over', but he also gives the name of the hawthorn in the sacred tree alphabet as 'uath' (meaning 'terror') and describes the tree as unlucky. The Romans considered it unlucky to marry in May, because it was a general period of sexual abstinence and purification before the licentious midsummer festival. Wearing new summer clothes in May would therefore be too early. Paradoxically, however, the month of May became associated from the 1st century BC with an aspect of the triple goddess, called Flora, whose orgiastic cult inspired young men and maidens to disappear into the spring woodlands whence 'few returned home undefiled' (see Barbara Walker's radical re-interpretation of myth in *Woman's Encyclopedia of Myths and Secrets*). 'Ne'er cast a clout till May is out' may therefore be a Puritan injunction against pagan sexual licence in the month of May, with its phallic maypoles and associated customs. Robert Graves points out that the saying is not necessarily connected with climate since it is also current in north-eastern Spain, where 'settled hot weather has come by Easter'.
Sara Jennett, Roath, Cardiff.

QUESTION: Can anyone throw light on the message: 'Thanks to St Jude for favours received' that appears in classified advertisements in newspapers?

☐ ROMAN Catholics believe that the saints in Heaven can intercede on our behalf with God in our prayers of petition as they, like us on Earth, are part of the Body of Christ that is the Church. For many centuries one saint, Jude, was neglected because of a confusion with Judas, the traitor who betrayed Jesus. Jude, like Judas, was one of the 12 Apostles and he even has a short Epistle included in the books of the New Testament. His intercession was only sought therefore when all else failed. He is therefore the patron saint 'of hopeless cases, of matters despaired of'. His devotees are keen to advertise his success to counteract his previous neglect. According to the *Roman Martyrology*, Jude was clubbed to death, I think in Persia. He is shown in pictures and statues carrying this club. He is also patron saint of policemen, no doubt the club in time reducing to a truncheon.
Anthony Jude Thurlow, Head of Religious Studies, Selby Tertiary College, Selby, N Yorks.

QUESTION: If Bob Dylan was born on May 24, 1941, how come the passport photograph accompanying the recent *Bootleg Series* album shows his date of birth as May 11, 1941?

☐ THE DISCREPANCY may reflect Dylan's wish to conceal his birth-date, which is of special interest to astrologers (of whom he is known to be wary). His birth certificate apparently records May 24 at 9.05 pm in Duluth, Minnesota – but was this tampered with? Alternatively, the 'bogus' passport date and height may reflect, in keeping with Dylan's image, the juxtaposition of an official 'lying' document with the 'real' person.
Neil Cooper, Brighton.

☐ IN A telephone interview with a New York radio station on May 21, 1986, he joked about putting his birthday back into June for that particular year, and on another occasion claimed that no one knew the real date he was born. The photograph is most probably an elaborate spoof, especially as he would need to stand on several copies of the new box-set to raise his height to the stated 5ft 11in.
Henry Porter, London SW18.

QUESTION: There is no zero in Roman numerals. Who invented zero, and when?

☐ THE ancient Greeks were aware of the concept of zero (as in 'We have *no* marbles'), but didn't think of it as a number. Aristotle had dismissed it because you couldn't divide by zero and get a down-to-earth result. The Romans never used their numerals for arithmetic, thus avoiding the need to keep a column empty with a zero symbol. Addition and subtraction were done instead on an abacus or counting frame. About 1,500 years ago in India a symbol was used to represent an abacus column with nothing in it. At first this was just a dot; later it became the '0' we know today. In the 8th century the great Arab mathematician, al-Khwarizmi, took it up and the Arabs eventually brought the zero to Europe. It wasn't warmly received; the Italians in particular were very suspicious of any change to their ancestors' system of numerals. In 1259 a law was passed forbidding bankers from using zero or any of the new Arab numerals in their accounts.
George Auckland and Martin Gorst, 'Away With Numbers',
BBC Television, London W5.

☐ A MONK called Abelard, who kept the accounts for a monastery in the West Midlands, heard of the new system

and went to Spain during the Moorish occupation. He converted to Islam and returned to his monastery after 20 years' study with the precious knowledge of nothing.
Dennis Salt, Horsham, W. Sussex.

□ MORE information can be found in chapter 7 of Professor Lancelot Hogben's book, *Mathematics for the Million.*
Leslie Farmelo, Shoreham-by-Sea, Sussex.

QUESTION: What makes the music for Hollywood Westerns instantly recognisable as such? Is there a basic musical formula or have our ears become conditioned?

□ WHETHER or not there is a basic formula, I was struck recently by the Allegro from Suite No. 2 of Respighi's *Ancient Airs and Dances.* To my (conditioned?) ears it sounds like typical Western soundtrack music. Since it is a 1926 orchestration of a piece written in the 17th century, the 'formula' could be quite old. Certainly music for sea/ocean scenes seems to have a style of its own, and any film with pictures of darkest outer space seems obliged to use music dominated by very low notes, usually played by synthesizer. Perhaps screen score-writers are just unoriginal.
John L. Birch, Buntingford, Herts.

□ MY THEORY is that because musical 'intervals' (the spaces between certain notes) convey emotional or stylised responses in clichéd music, the intervals of a fourth and fifth convey feelings of open space: prairies, deserts, etc. Aaron Copland's music for *Billy the Kid* is typical of this. Many film composers follow trends set by established composers and you will find that the slushy, romantic music in films is often similar to that of, say Mahler or Bruckner. In sentimental pop or rock ballads much is made of the 'suspension' (carrying a melody note over moving chords) which carries emotional responses. As for the fast music in Westerns, it is often developed from American folk tunes (Dvorak's 'New World' symphony is a classic example) and the rhythmic, moody music connected with Red Indians is also a sort of poor relation to their folk tradition. In the end, it's simply because composers follow trends and write similar music, but I hope the technical answers I've given may be of some help.

Peter S. Jones, Wallasey, Merseyside.

☐ AS ONE of the key elements of the Western is the horse, most pieces of music have the tempo of the horse (or horses) figuring on the screen. 'Gallop' music often appears in chase scenes. The Indian also have horse tempo music, but it is invariably louder to match what are usually their collective aggressive designs on wagon trains, etc. Other groups blessed with their own mood music include Mexican bandits and the US Cavalry. The other Western style is 'vast landscape' music. The themes from *The Big Country*, Tiomkin's *Giant* and *Shane*, or Bernstein's *The Magnificent Seven* are prime examples. There is no doubt that there are recognised Western chord structures as well as instrumentation. A slow, lazy, acoustic guitar picking on the chords of C major, C sharp diminished, D minor and G seventh, for example, will remind us of a walking horse, as will a lazy A major followed by a B minor and E seventh (e.g. *Shane*).

Trevor Popple, Redhill, Surrey.

QUESTION: A levels are often said to be poor predictors of degree results. Is there any evidence for this?

☐ THE FIRST thing we show new students in our department is a chart of the previous summer's degree results plotted against A level scores. It looks as though somebody has fired a shotgun at it, with very poor correlation between the two,

and we say: 'It's all still to play for.' The poor correlation is not necessarily a criticism of A levels: quality of teaching, parental pressure, interest in the subject, etc, all vary from student to student and between school and college.

(Dr) M. H. Ford-Smith, School of Chemistry and Molecular Sciences, University of Sussex.

☐ WHEN I was a lecturer in civil engineering at a polytechnic, a colleague investigated the relation between the O level and A level qualifications of past students and the final aggregate mark they achieved for their degree. He was surprised to find little constant correlation between degree marks and the type of A levels that the students had, but there was a close correlation with the number and quality of their O level results.

W. G. A. Gardner, Shanklin, Isle of Wight.

☐ SOME years ago I compared students' grades in English at A level with their results in the subject in the first year in finals examinations. Of those with an A in English, 80 per cent achieved honours standard in their first-year examinations. Not all of these read English, but of those who did, 90 per cent got good honours degrees. Of those with B or C in

English, 50 per cent achieved honours standard in their first year; the percentage was about the same for either grade. Again, not all of these read for honours, but of those who did, only about 50 per cent got good honours degrees. I concluded that A levels are not bad predictors of degree results.

James Ogden, Senior Lecturer, Department of English, University College of Wales, Aberystwyth.

☐ ALMOST certainly yes, but no one can do the experiment needed to confirm this. It would require assigning university places to A level candidates at random (rather than by A level grades). This would ensure any calculation included lots of Ds and Es as well as all the As and Bs comprising the current student sample. Currently we have a problem statisticians call 'restricted range'. While one side of the co-relationship (degree mark) has lots of variability, variability on the other side (A level grades) is narrowly confined to the top end. However, the correspondents above who can only use this creamed-off sample are still making a useful point in reporting no correlation with degree results. Having wisely privileged the As and Bs, admissions tutors should look for other indicators that allow them to make finer judgements within this (increasingly large) sample.

Charles Crook, Dept of Psychology, University of Durham.

☐ THERE have been several studies. The usual measurement is a correlation between 0 and 1 (where 0 means no relationship and 1 means a perfect relationship). Typically, a correlation of between .3 and .4 has emerged, though in some subjects, like mathematics, it may be a little higher. If you square a correlation you get what is called the 'common factor variance' (i.e. what the two measures appear to have in common, the extent to which the one appears to 'predict' or 'explain' the variance in another). The A level grades only 'explain' 9 to 16 per cent of the variation in degree class. In the 1970s there were attempts to improve the prediction of degree success by developing a Test of Academic Aptitude. Unfortunately its predictive power, a correlation of just over .3, was no better than that of A levels, so it never came into use. There are, however, two problems with correlations as a form of prediction. The first is 'outliers' – people who lie outside the main trend. The lower the correlation the more of these there are and the less meaningful any prediction will be. The second is an artefact which occurs when correlations are used within a narrow band of the whole spectrum, known as 'homogeneity of variance'. Most studies of university students are looking at people in a very thin band at the top of the ability range, the majority of whom got A, B or C at A level and then went on to get an upper or lower second class degree. If the whole population took A levels, and then the whole population went on to a degree, the correlation might well be .7 or .8 but I can't see that experiment being tried! In summary, A level may not be a brilliant predictor but it is better than it seems.

(Prof) E. C. Wragg, School of Education, University of Exeter.

QUESTION: In a restaurant, when do you become legally liable to pay the bill? Is it when you place your order, when the food is served, or when it is eaten?

☐ YOU become liable as soon as the contract is 'substantially performed'. You could keep two teams of lawyers happy for hours discussing precisely when this moment happens if you were prepared to pay for the privilege. More useful questions to ask would be: what is the last instant at which you can withdraw from the transaction without liability of any kind (answer: the instant before you order); and if you can be proved to have intended not to pay, what actions expose you to criminal liability (answer: just about anything, though the precise moment at which you develop this intent will determine whether the appropriate charge is obtaining property by deception, obtaining services by deception,

evading liability by deception, or simply making off without payment)?
Steve Hedley, Fellow in Law, Christ's College, Cambridge.

☐ IT WOULD appear that you become liable to pay before any of these. I have had the misfortune to pay a bill for a meal not having ordered, been served, or actually having eaten it. As soon as you make a reservation to eat a meal (or presumably step into a restaurant to eat one) you implicitly make a legal contract.
Mark Bridle, Southampton.

☐ THE question was discussed in a case in the 1930s, which I recall as Lockett v Charles. The guest at a restaurant meal was taken ill afterwards and sued the restaurant. This was before the 'snail in the ginger beer bottle' case (Donoghue v Stevenson), so everything turned on whether there was a contract, to which the Sale of Goods Act, 1893, applied, between the guest and the restaurant. The High Court held that the contract was made when the orders were placed, and that where two people go to a restaurant and place orders, the implication is that each becomes liable to pay for the food ordered by himself. This may be rebutted where the host has booked the table and indicated he will be entertaining guests. But the principle seems to be established: the contract is made when the orders are given. However, contracts made by conduct are notoriously difficult to define. So far as I know, the courts have not yet decided at what point the contract is made when a person boards a bus.
John Paris, Abingdon, Oxfordshire.

QUESTION: Why does Michelangelo's Moses sport a devilish set of horns?

☐ IT'S BECAUSE of a mistranslation of the Hebrew text into the Vulgate, the version of the Bible from which Michelan-

gelo gained his knowledge of Moses. The text (Exodus 34, v 29, 30, and 35) actually says Moses's face was 'shining' when he came down from the presence of God on Mount Sinai where he had been given the Ten Commandments. In Hebrew, the verb 'qâran' meaning shining, is similar to the word 'qérén' meaning horned. The confusion arose because Hebrew was written without vowels, so the word would have been written as 'qrn' in either case.
G. W. Eggins, Nailsea, Bristol.

☐ FROM the 12th century to the 15th, the portrayal of a horned Moses was almost *de rigueur*. It was not abandoned until the 16th century, and then more from a fear of Protestant sarcasm than in the interests of scholarship.
John Edwards, Oxford.

QUESTION: Why is it considered abnormal to write in green ink?

☐ IN CELTIC mythology a letter written in green ink represents a harbinger of bad luck (see, for example, the writings of the 18th-century Irish poet, Hugh O'Neill).
Finlay McInally, London SE1.

☐ AS A YOUNG bank clerk in 1975 I was forbidden to use green ink because this was the colour used by the bank's inspectors. Any document bearing a green counter-signature (or more usually a squiggle) was judged to have passed through their audit. Accordingly anything not marked in green was still the subject of scrutiny. Fortunately I was not there long enough to develop too many negative associations with green ink. Occasionally, as an act of minor deviancy, I write cheques in green ink.
S. J. Welch, Sheffield.

QUESTION: Who is, or was, Natalie Kalmus and why is she listed as colour director in the credits of just about every Technicolor film made in the US or Britain before the mid-1960s?

☐ SHE WAS the wife of Dr Herbert T. Kalmus, founder of the Technicolor company. For many years she was the senior colour consultant for the organisation, while Dr Kalmus concentrated on the development of new film stocks and cameras. Early Technicolor systems – including two-strip, three-strip, and Monopack – were unable to resolve colours naturally, and it was the function of the colour consultant to recommend changes to costumes, make-up, and set designs in order to display Technicolor to its best advantage. The use of a colour consultant was compulsory, and resented by many studios. Mrs Kalmus had the power to make sweeping changes to any production on which she worked. Dr and Mrs Kalmus parted in 1948, when Natalie sued her partner for half his fortune as a divorce settlement. The case was thrown out of court when it was revealed that the Kalmuses had secretly divorced in 1919 and never remarried. The name of Natalie Kalmus disappeared from Technicolor films after 1950, to be replaced by a credit for the actual consultant provided by the company.
Bob Richardson, Northolt.

☐ DETERMINED that Technicolor should never be seen to anything but the very best advantage, Mrs Kalmus saw to it that all sets, costumes, and lighting fully accommodated her husband's colour process. Not all her collaborators appreciated being dictated to in this way. One of her victims, the distinguished cameraman, James Wong Howe, was barred from working with Technicolor for 10 years after employing less than the stipulated levels of lighting on the cave sequences in *The Adventures Of Tom Sawyer* (1938).
Richard Chatten, London E17.

QUESTION: There used to be a BBC television rock music programme called *The Old Grey Whistle Test*. What is the origin of this title?

☐ IT DATES back to the days of Tin Pan Alley, when music publishing companies would literally employ songwriters, working in the building on a 9 to 5 basis, turning out songs on a kind of 'hit factory' conveyor belt. The Brill Building in New York, where Neil Sedaka, Carole King, Gerry Goffin, Ellie Greenwich and many more writers provided the charts with so many stunning songs in the late 1950s and early 1960s was possibly the definitive example. What they were looking for were songs with a catchy chorus that could be hummed or whistled after the first time of hearing. At the end of a working week, the songs deemed to be the strongest were played to an in-house gathering of the 'general public' – the peripheral staff employed as maybe cleaners or doormen around the building. These people were known by the nickname the 'Old Greys' at that time. If, after hearing a song only once or twice, they were able to hum or whistle along to the chorus, the song was deemed to have the greatest chance of making the charts because it passed The Old Grey Whistle Test. The phrase became general currency in the music business at that time. As to its literal application on the programme . . . well, we broke the rules. Many of the bands we featured during the mid-70s would have been embarrassed to have achieved success in the singles market at that time. Alex Harvey and Captain Beefheart hardly turned out top 40 songs on a regular basis.
Bob Harris, BBC Radio 1 (presenter of The Old Grey Whistle Test, *1972-79).*

☐ THE programme's founder, Mike Appleton, chose the title in an era when cumbersome and meaningless names (like Monty Python's Flying Circus and Sgt Pepper's Lonely Hearts Club Band) were all the rage.
*Trevor Dann (*Whistle Test *producer 1984-87), London W1.*

QUESTION: Why do flamingos stand on one leg?

☐ THE LEGS and feet of these birds have a high surface-area-to-mass ratio. They are therefore susceptible to heat loss, particularly if the bird stands still for long periods with its feet and legs in water. Many water birds have thus evolved the habit of standing with one leg tucked up into the feathers of the lower body, reducing the potential heat loss by 50 per cent.

Ian White, Bolton, Lancs.

QUESTION: Are there rhyming slangs in other languages?

☐ WHILE working in the south of France I was travelling in a car driven by a Frenchman when we were 'cut up' by someone in another car with the immatriculation number 75 (Paris). My friend called out of the window: 'Tête de chien.' When I asked what he meant by this, he replied: 'Un Parisien!'

Robert Martin, East Kilbride.

☐ THE CANTONESE dialect of Chinese uses rhyming slang. Here are two examples: Mid-autumn festival, on the 15th day of the 8th month of the lunar calendar, is celebrated by worshipping the moon, burning lanterns and eating special cakes known as yuet beng. In English these are known as 'moon cakes', which sounds very like the Cantonese *moon gik* ('extremely boring'). Hence the Cantonese phrase for an extremely boring thing or person, *gweilo yuet beng* ('foreign devils' moon cake'). In another example, the Cantonese refer to those they regard as detestable as *fei jau woh seung* (literally, 'African monk'). Although at first glance this phrase seems derogatory, it actually contains no racial connotations, deriving instead from the similarity of pronunciation between its alternative, *hak yan jang* (literally 'black monk') and *hat yan jang* ('detestable or disgusting'). *Tim Doling, Pokfulam, Hong Kong.*

QUESTION: Our son insists on cracking his fingers. What makes the noise inside his hands, and is he likely to suffer in the future?

☐ THE lowering of pressure in the synovial fluid which fills each joint causes it to boil, briefly, and the bubble of vapour collapses with a 'crack' – or so current theories suggest. It may be that the cartilaginous surfaces are minutely damaged by the process, in which case habitual knuckle-cracking could be related to joint problems in later life. That, though conjecture, makes enough sense to warn against too much of the habit. *Brian J. Ford, London SW1.*

QUESTION: What is the longest voyage ever made by a pedalo?

☐ IN THE book, *Wagstaffe the Wind-Up Boy*, by Jan Needle, the hero goes round the Isle of Wight for £5. When the author visited our school last year, he said it was based on a true event, although my dad does not believe him. Anyway, I do. *William Gardner (aged 11), Didsbury, Manchester.*

☐ IN 1970 David Brickwood, an industrial designer, and Derek Rothera, an accountant, pedaloed from Dover to Audruxelles (about 25 miles north of Boulogne) – an estimated distance of 50 miles. The support boat, driven by myself and A. Lamb, turned back with steering trouble after two hours. The pedalo reached Audruxelles at 5.30 a.m. after a 16-hour crossing. *Roger Mutton, London E1.*

QUESTION: What happened at Montpellier around the beginning of the last century that resulted in the name of this French provincial town being used for so many Regency houses, squares, streets, etc, in England?

☐ A BOOK by George Savage, *Languedoc*, explains: 'In the 18th century Montpellier possessed a flourishing English colony but this was in the process of being removed to Beziers before the revolution started in 1789. During the Napoleonic wars English residents in France were interned here and they found life so congenial that when they returned to England and went to live in places like Kensington, Hove and Cheltenham, they named streets, crescents and squares after Montpellier.'
(Mrs) D. G. Ousey, Great Shelford, Cambridge.

☐ MONTPELLIER, seat of an ancient university and medical school and virtually the only malaria-free cultural centre on the Mediterranean, was a favourite destination for young British aristocrats and their tutors doing the Grand Tour of Europe during the 17th and early 18th centuries. By the early 19th century, when the British streets were built, Montpellier was no longer favoured by well-heeled British tourists, who were transferring their affections to Nice and Monte Carlo, but the aristocratic association persisted and the speculative builders and developers who 'ran up' the new terraces and streets for their middle class clients naturally chose an upmarket name with aristocratic pretensions — much as new housing estates today are given grandiose names redolent of the Victorian country house. What is unclear is why invariably the street name is misspelt 'Montpelier'(one L), unless the builders were trying to save a little on the cast iron of the street signage.
(Dr) Iain Stevenson, London WC2.

QUESTION: How can I weigh my head?

☐ FILL a water butt until water flows out of the overflow. Let the water settle and then immerse the head completely, keeping it submerged until the water level has settled, having first arranged some method of collecting the displaced water that will flow out of the overflow. The volume of water displaced should then be measured and the experiment repeated, this time immersing the whole body. Again the volume of displaced water should be recorded. The ratio of the first volume to the second, multiplied by total body weight gives the proportion of body weight that is due to the head. This method assumes the human body has a uniform density and does not take into account the contribution of any pegs on the nose needed to prevent drowning.
(Dr) N. J. Mason, University of Oxford.

☐ DR MASON'S method does not allow for the dense nature of the head, which contains much bone. A more accurate method is to float in the barrel, adjusting your lung volume to leave the head completely out of the water. While holding your breath, top up the barrel to the overflow and then submerge completely, collecting the displaced water, and measuring its volume. Climb out of the barrel, without further spillage, and then refill the barrel, measuring the volume needed. The floating volume of the body (the volume to keep the head up) can be calculated from the difference of the two volumes measured above. The weight of the head is the floating volume (in litres) less the body weight (in kilos).
J. B. Diamond, Hertford.

☐ J. B. DIAMOND'S formula yields a head weight of zero, which cannot be right, even in J. B. Diamond's case.
M J Lloyd, London EC1.

☐ FIND a long board with pivotal centre mounting (e.g. a see-saw): weigh yourself unclothed, then lie on the board

with the pivotal point coinciding with the base of the skull. Have someone place weights on the head end of the board up to a distance not exceeding the length from the pivot to the heels in the opposite direction. When the see-saw is balanced, deduct the sum of the added weights from your total body weight to obtain the weight of your head.
Jane Pepper, Canterbury.

☐ ENTERTAINING but wrong. If it worked, so would perpetual motion. An approximate answer would be got with the aid of muscle relaxant, a gravity meter, and a blow from Michael Watson. But for a less dramatic method, take a seesaw, a ruler, and a large inanimate object. Balance flat on your back on the seesaw, then bend your head forward on to your chest. The seesaw will tilt: shuffle along to restore the balance. Measure the distance you have to shuffle and divide this by the amount by which you moved (the centre of) your head. This gives the weight of your head as a fraction of your whole body weight.
Peter Green, Department of Mathematics, University of Bristol.

☐ PETER GREEN gives a neat answer but I am left wondering what to do with the 'large inanimate object'. Here is an alternative solution that, again, assumes you can estimate the position of the centre of gravity of the head. Take a plank longer than your body and place it across two weighing scales that act as pivotal points. Lie along the plank with head to the left of the left pivot, and move the right pivot until it reads the same as the left one. (Each reading will equal half the combined weight of body and plank.) Saw off and weigh a length of plank to the right so that the shortened plank overhangs each pivot equally. The weight of the head is equal to the weight of this off-cut multiplied by the distance of the centre of gravity of the head from the left pivot and divided by the distance from the centre of the off-cut to the right pivot.
Rob Johnsey, Redditch, Worcs.

INDEX